D0760309

The Primary Curriculum
Design Handbook

Also available from Continuum

Creating Tomorrow's Schools Today, Richard Gerver
Leading the Sustainable School, Debra Massey
New Primary Leaders, edited by Michael Cowie
Tales from the Head's Room, Mike Kent

The Primary Curriculum Design Handbook

Preparing Our Children for the 21st Century

Brian Male

continuum

Continuum International Publishing Group

The Tower Building	80 Maiden Lane
11 York Road	Suite 704
London SE1 7NX	New York NY 10038

www.continuumbooks.com

British Library Cataloguing-in-Publication Data
A catalogue record for this book is available from the British Library.

ISBN: 978-1-4411-2569-9 (paperback)

Library of Congress Cataloging-in-Publication Data
A catalog record for this book is available from the Library of Congress.
Male, Brian.
    The primary curriculum design handbook : preparing our children for the
    21st century / Brian Male.
      p. cm.
      Includes bibliographical references and index.
      ISBN 978-1-4411-2569-9 (pbk.)
1. Education, Elementary–Curricula–Great Britain. 2. Curriculum planning–Great Britain. I. Title.

    LB1564.G7M35 2012
    372.19–dc23

2011022991

Typeset by Newgen Imaging Systems Pvt Ltd, Chennai, India
Printed and bound in India

Contents

SECTION III: **How will we know if we are successful?**

SECTION IV: **How do we get from here to there?**

Foreword

When a school designs its curriculum, it is setting out the very essence of its work. What do we want the young people who learn here to experience, to know, to be able to do? What sort of people are we trying to help them to become? What role does our school take in the process of helping these young people to grow? How do we help their parents to nurture them, which in some cases will mean topping up an idyllic childhood and at the other extreme providing some of the very basics of life? The school tries to organise the learning experience to make maximum use of every moment for every child.

Using every moment means that the curriculum is more than the timetable of lessons. It is what happens in the day-to-day life of the school: taking part in assembly, using the library or enjoying the school grounds. The curriculum also includes the things children see as big events: the residential visit, the sports tournament or the school production. Many schools call this extra-curricular activity, yet the reality is that these events are at the heart of the learning that many adults remember from their own school days. They are the times when their learning came to life and made sense because it had a real context.

Designing this learning experience for children through a primary experience of several years is an exciting, yet daunting, challenge. The physical growth of children through the primary phase is amazing; how do we help their intellect to grow at the same rate while at the same time nurturing their social and emotional outlooks and giving them that personal spirit to influence their own lives?

Brian Male brings his considerable experience to the challenge of helping each school to design the curriculum that matters for their children. He draws out the difference between curriculum design and planning and shows how the principles that underlie our aims for the children should be the driving force for our learning offer. Brian draws on his experience in QCA's review of curriculum, and his work as a consultant to Unesco to show how people across the world are thinking about how to make learning matter to children at the start of the second millennium. What also shines through is Brian's deep commitment to primary education.

This handbook of curriculum design is readable and thought provoking and prompts discussion and decision at every level in the school. The examples of learning, all from time Brian has spent with teachers and children in schools, show the vitality of learning where it matters most as it meets the child.

The handbook appears at a fascinating time in English education. The wholesale review of national curriculum brings debate about what is in and what is out of the content. Brian's book shows how the content is but one piece of the jigsaw and that complex argument about basics and knowledge and skills might serve as time and energy traps. The clever school will use this book alongside the developing national agenda to ensure that the principles of learning are clear and understood by everyone. In that way, the curriculum design at school level will meet the national requirements as well as meet the needs of the children we teach.

Enjoy this book, talk about it, use it as a basis for work with parents and children and design the curriculum that helps children to cross thresholds in the learning journey. The curriculum should be treasured. This book will show you how it can be treasured by the people who need the best we can offer; the budding mathematicians, young geographers, fledgling historians and novice artists in our schools. They will go on to be archivists, inventors, builders, designers, actors, gardeners . . . and decent adults.

Mick Waters
Professor of Education
University of Wolverhampton, UK

Introduction

Think of the curriculum as a forecast of possibilities within an arena of opportunities.

– Carla Rinaldi, President of Reggio Children in Reggio Emilia, Italy and professor at the University of Modena and Reggio Emilia – quoted from a conference speech in London, 2006

This is a curriculum design handbook, not a curriculum planning handbook. Curriculum design is about all the things we want children to learn; it is also about creating all the experiences that children need in order to learn those things. It is about ensuring that those experiences are effective and compelling in themselves, and also that the sum total of those experiences adds up to a coherent and worthwhile programme that will bring about the ends that we seek. The accumulation of all these experiences is the curriculum itself.

This is a primary school curriculum design handbook. The examples are taken mainly from schools following the English Primary National Curriculum, but the principles of design apply to any age in any country. English primary schools have to take account of both the primary and the Early Years Foundation Stage (EYFS) curriculum and while the focus of this book is primary, the principles are universal.

The primary school is a time of rapid change and development for children. It is much more than an interlude between the Nursery and Secondary School. It is a time for establishing the basis of attitudes and values, skills, knowledge and understanding that will last a lifetime. It is a time for children to establish their own identity as human beings, to find out how they relate to other people in a much wider society, and to begin to comprehend what it means to be a global citizen. It is a time for exploring and making connections between a rich variety of practical experiences; a time when direct experiences are put together into conceptual development; a time for children to develop imaginatively and creatively; a time for children to be excited, challenged and inspired; a time to lay down the roots to lifelong learning. It is a time for children to be children.

Curriculum design is about how we can construct a curriculum that will match these aspirations.

This book is being published just as the English National Curriculum is under review. So some English schools might consider this to be an inopportune time to be thinking about the curriculum at all: What's the point of thinking about the curriculum when they are going to change it all anyway? But there is a very good reason for doing so.

The curriculum of schools is much more than a national curriculum. Schools are rich in learning, much of which goes way beyond any national curriculum, and there is a set of principles and approaches that will take a curriculum way beyond the ordinary and sufficient, and make it truly 'world-class'. These principles and approaches apply in any country whatever the national curriculum. They take learning beyond the national and towards the universal, and they will enable schools to incorporate the revised English national expectations into a truly inspiring curriculum for children.

These world-class principles are about the way a country's national curriculum is turned into learning experiences for children that are exciting and uplifting, that recognise the individuality of every child, and which encourage their development as human beings. These principles underpin this book, and provide a way in which the curriculum can be made exciting and uplifting whatever the national curriculum is, or turns out to be. The principles are about how the school can add value to national expectations and locate them in a setting that is both local and global.

These principles can be applied to the present English National Curriculum, and to any new one that might be devised. They can be applied to the national curriculum of any country, and provide a way of taking national requirements and using them to create learning that is exciting, coherent and fulfilling; learning that will prepare young people for the 21st century.

This is not an academic book, although it is based on research and makes reference to it. It is a practical book for curriculum designers. It does not provide a ready-made, off the peg, or off the web curriculum that will apply in all schools. But it provides a route to designing a curriculum that can challenge and inspire all learners, whatever their background or ability.

It sees the role of the teacher as more than a deliverer of someone else's curriculum, more than technicians rehashing someone else's recipes. We must unleash the power of the curriculum by enabling teachers to be curriculum designers who create learning experiences that excite and engage the children; experiences that are rooted in their present understandings, but that widen their horizons and raise their aspirations.

Headteachers have the key role in curriculum design, for it is they who must be flexible in order to ensure that the curriculum builds on what children have just learned and responds to their developing interests and needs, while also providing a coherent curriculum over the six primary years. It also needs to be a curriculum that excites imaginations and provides inspiration. It should be a feast of learning that no child can resist.

We need a curriculum with a strong moral purpose; a curriculum that we all came into the profession to teach. If we get this right, we can send every young person out into adulthood with the confidence, the ability and the desire to make the world a better place.

SECTION I

How do we design a curriculum?

1 Curriculum design

The Fruit Machine Company

Despite its name, the Fruit Machine Company makes and sells snacks. It has a strong moral commitment to healthy eating and a sustainable environment. It is a not-for-profit company in the sense that it is actually run by volunteers who take neither pay nor dividends. But they are all particularly keen to make a profit that they can use for good causes within a school. The volunteers are 10-year-old children in an English primary school, and their Company sells to their fellow pupils.

By the first morning break, these children have already taken delivery of the stock, cut up melons and other fruit into slices, prepared cheese on crackers and set out the stall. The deliveries are logged and the accounts prepared. The children have worked out how much to charge for each slice and snack, and portion control has been established so that a profit is assured. Hygiene and safety are accounted for. Selling is the end of a long process.

The company is a regular and ongoing part of school life. They have to confront issues about waste, and work out the optimum amounts to buy. They have to cope with seasonal variations in price when the customer is resistant to paying more. They keep meticulous records on a spreadsheet and pore over the accounts looking for ways to improve profits. They draw up rotas to operate the stall, design publicity, improve their efficiency, make good relationships with their suppliers, check the quality of incoming produce and insist on high standards. Welcome to the world of the Fruit Machine Company.

All too frequently, the primary curriculum has become constrained by the very plans we draw up to frame it. Instead of unleashing the excitement and curiosity of young children it can become a seemingly endless list of things to get through. This book is about how we can cut through this, and create the exciting, engaging and spontaneous curriculum we all want. A curriculum that is able to respond to children's interests and needs, yet able to ensure the highest of standards.

What is the secret of such magic? It is a tree.

How can a tree do all this? Read on.

What does the Fruit Machine Company have to do with a book about designing a curriculum? Surely these are 'extra-curricular' activities, and so not part of the curriculum at all? But when you think about it, an amazing amount of learning is packed into running this company: English, maths, science, citizenship, all of which is part of the usual curriculum anyway. What might be different here is the way in which these things were learned. None of it was explicitly planned by the teacher in advance, and very little took place in 'lessons'. Yet it is all part of these young people's learning experiences. And it was there by design. Designed, but not planned.

More than planning

Curriculum design is about more than listing all the things we want children to learn; it is also about designing the experiences that children need in order to learn those things. It is about ensuring that those experiences are effective and compelling in themselves, and also that the sum total of those experiences adds up to a coherent and worthwhile programme that will bring about the ends that we seek.

The curriculum is the whole set of learning experiences that children are involved in as they move through the school.

There are three levels of understanding the curriculum:

- The curriculum set out by the nation: all those things the nation thinks our young people should learn;
- The curriculum set out by the school or the teacher: the mediation of those national expectations into a form that is relevant to the particular children in the school or class;
- The curriculum as experienced by the children: which might vary from child to child even within a class.

The first two levels impact upon the third. We need to consider all three levels, but what really counts is what the children actually learn.

More than the national curriculum

The nation sets out what it wants its children to learn in a national curriculum. The school interprets this and sets out what it wants its pupils to learn in its curriculum plans. But success depends on what the children make of all this: it is their set of experiences that determines what they will learn. And this can vary from child to child even within the same class or lesson, because they all bring something different to their learning, and are building on a different past set of experiences. They are all seeking to make sense of new information in the light of their present understandings, and those present understandings will vary from child to child.

The curriculum of every school is much more than the national curriculum – whatever country you are in. A national curriculum prescribes a common set of learning to which all children are entitled. But these expectations are always mediated by the school itself, and each school responds to national expectations in its own way – even if they all think they are responding in the same way. And the national expectations need to be placed in the local context and presented in such a way that they make sense to the particular set of children. The national expectations are always achieved within a local setting. But what are these national expectations and how do we build them into the curriculum?

More than 'the basics'

When they start primary school at the age of 4, children are still at the brink of life. A vast, new and exciting world is there for them to explore, and they are still developing as human beings who are about find themselves within that world. The primary school curriculum must help open that world to them. To do this, it must provide experiences that are extensive and expansive. It must equip them with the skills they need to find their way around that world, and find their place within it.

Children do not start entirely afresh on this journey, although we would not want to lose this freshness. Other human beings have gone before them and have left their trail of accumulated knowledge and experience. People have already constructed ways of trying to understand the world. Children need to be made aware of this accumulated wisdom, and to be aware of how it has been organised into categories, domains or subject areas. A key role of the primary curriculum is to help children come to terms with what has already been found out about the world, without dampening their desire to find out for themselves.

To navigate this accumulated wisdom and to make their own discoveries, children need to be equipped to do so. They need personal qualities to enable them to be confident and resilient in the journey, and social skills to co-operate with others along the way. They need cognitive skills to make sense of all the information they will find. They need to acquire a facility with the key methods that are used in discovery: basic communication, ability to understand the world through basic mathematics, and ability to use basic technology to do so. These are the basics. But they are not ends in themselves; they are ways of enabling children to explore their world. The curriculum must equip children with these basics, so that they can do much more.

It can take some time for children to acquire these basics, but this need not delay the journey. Well designed experiences can enable children to develop the basic skills and qualities they need as the journey unfolds. Developing skills in the context where they are needed enhances both the skills and the context. It also maintains the freshness of learning and the joy of discovery.

This picture of children exploring their world may sound rather fanciful put this way, but it represents an understanding of children as actively engaged in making meaning. This understanding has been developed from Piaget (1969) through Vygotsky (1978) to more recent researchers such as Goswami (2008).

More than subjects

What children learn in primary school goes way beyond the subjects on the timetable. They are learning all the time, whether we want them to or not, and by the age of 11 they are very different people from the 4-year-olds who started in the reception class. This breadth of learning is often reflected in our school's aims which almost always refer to aspects of personal, social and emotional development, and to a range of skills.

Personal development

Most countries make reference to personal development in their national curricula and some set specific targets. In England, the 'Early Years Foundation Stage' (EYFS) guidance for children up to the age of 5 details aspects of personal development, but there is no corresponding statutory section in the primary national curriculum. However, it is part of the non-statutory guidance as 'Personal, Social and Health Education' and Citizenship (PSHCE), and schools and parents see it as an important part of the work of the school.

Key skills

Most countries also make reference to a range of skills that apply across subjects and go beyond them. These might be general, such as critical thinking, problem solving, communicating or investigating, or they might be more specific such as analysing, synthesising and evaluating. Because they apply across the curriculum, these are often referred to as 'generic skills' or 'Key Skills'. The English National Curriculum lists six 'Key Skills' and five 'Thinking Skills' but they are not always built into the school curriculum in a way that integrates them into other learning and ensures their systematic development. In fact, they are seldom built into the school curriculum at all, and few people seem to know they exist. (Did you know that they exist? Could you list them? The answer is in Chapter 2!)

More than knowledge

Within the subjects themselves, there can be a tension between subject knowledge, skills and understanding. These three terms have always been used in the English National Curriculum to denote different forms of learning:

- *Knowledge* is the possession of information
- A *skill* is the ability to perform an operation (either mental or physical). It is basically the ability to do something.
- *Understanding* goes beyond knowledge into a comprehension of general principles that allow pieces of knowledge to be fitted into a structure. These structures are often referred to as 'concepts'.

Much of the debate about the importance of knowledge arises because the term 'knowledge' is used in a variety of ways in education: from 'knowing that' (simple information to be recalled) to 'knowing how to' (which implies skills) and 'knowing about' (which implies understanding). There is general agreement that conceptual development (understanding) is at the deepest level of learning.

A simple example would be a child learning about capital cities. The ability to recall that Paris is the capital city of France is a piece of knowledge. The ability to find out what a country's capital city is, if you did not already know, would involve a skill (using an atlas or the internet). Explaining why one city rather than another is the capital (Why is Sydney not the capital of Australia?) involves understanding the concept of capitals. There is a further dimension to learning: the extent of your knowledge about capitals (depth as well as range).

It is important to note here two things: first that the distinction between knowledge, skills and understanding is key to curriculum design because they each involve a different type of learning that the curriculum needs to take account of, and, second, the curriculum must involve more than knowledge. A curriculum without skills or understanding would be pointlessly shallow. It would be curriculum of the pub quiz. A curriculum without knowledge would be equally pointless, and it would also be impossible!

Putting them together: competencies

When education is successful, the learners are able to make use of the knowledge, understanding and skills they have acquired because they have developed the right attitudes and approaches to use them effectively. This coming together of knowledge, understanding, skills and personal development is usually referred to as a 'competency'. Many countries make use of this concept in developing their curricula. For example, the Singapore National Curriculum (and remember that Singapore always does well on international comparisons) has at its heart: 'Social and Emotional Competencies' and '21st Century Competencies'. Singapore's 21st century competencies are listed as:

- Civic literacy,
- Global awareness
- Cross-curricular skills
- Critical and media skills
- Information and communication skills

The key to curriculum design is how these three aspects – subject knowledge, personal development and key skills – can be brought together for their mutual benefit and to achieve competency. It is not a matter of 'either subjects or skills'. It is both – and personal development as well. At the heart of curriculum design is the methodology for putting these together.

More than lessons

The key reason why a school's curriculum is inevitably broader than a national curriculum is that most curriculum planning focuses on what goes on in lessons, and children do not learn only in lessons. They learn from the *routines* of the school, the things that happen every day or week such as changing library books, going to assembly, looking after plants, lunchtimes and breaks, performing duties, organising resources and tidying up. Some of these routines can be rich sources of learning, such as the Fruit Machine Company. Sometimes schools are oblivious to all this learning and it can even run counter to their intentions. In other cases, they build it into their design and channel the learning profitably.

In addition to the routines, schools frequently organise *events*: things which do not happen every day or week. These can be of long continuous duration such as a residential visit or an Arts Week, or short such as a visit to a Museum, or over a long period of time like putting on a school play. Unlike the routines, these usually are planned as part of the overt curriculum.

There are also all those things that happen *outside of normal hours*. They may not involve all the children all the time, but a huge amount of learning takes place in clubs, societies, sports, music groups, gardening clubs, school councils and environment committees. These are seldom part of the planned curriculum, but are another rich source of learning.

There is also the *ethos* of the school and the set of *relationships* that prevail. These are not part of the planned curriculum, but will impact upon it, especially when the list of things we want children to learn includes things like: 'show respect', or 'be sensitive to others' or 'be tolerant and sensitive to others' needs'. This can impact on the school as a 'learning community' where both adults and other children contribute to learning (Lave & Wenger 1991).

The point is not that a full curriculum *should* look like this, but that the curriculum of a primary school *inevitably* looks like this. There will be very few schools indeed where all these things do not go on. It is just that we tend to focus on the lessons. If we were to draw a map of the things that make up the curriculum the map might look something like the one shown in Figure 1.1.

Do these things go on in your school? Are there other things too? What would the relative size of the different boxes be in your school? (You don't need to do this exactly with a calendar and stop-watch – just note down your overall impression.) Would the map be the same for each class? Is this the best ratio for producing the learning you want? Most schools find that the map changes significantly across the year groups. A map of the Early Years curriculum is much higher on routines, events and other activities, and the lesson boxes look far smaller. By Year 6, lessons tend to dominate.

Of course, learning does not happen in separate boxes. The impact on children is a holistic one. If we can get our curriculum design right, we can harness the power of all these apparently separate boxes to maximise the learning for each child. We need to break down the walls and benefit from the flow of learning.

In most schools, lessons tend to be the main vehicle of learning, but lessons come in a wide variety of forms. It is essential to consider these as part of curriculum design, and we shall do so in later chapters. But curriculum design also needs to take account of the totality of learning in the school, the balance between the different elements, and which type of learning experience is most suited to promoting different kinds of learning. All of this

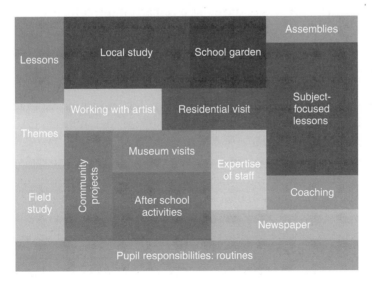

Figure 1.1 The primary school curriculum

impacts on whether our curriculum is successful in bringing about the ends that we seek. This, in turn, brings us to the first of the three design questions, and until we know the answer to this question we cannot expect to be able to design a worthwhile curriculum. What ends are we seeking? (If this is the first design question, what are the other two?)

What are we trying to achieve?

You might think that there is no point is asking such a question because we have a National Curriculum, and our job is to teach it, or to 'cover' it, or 'deliver' it. The National Curriculum has its own aims, so we all know what we are trying to achieve anyway. Or do we? Is it really so clear-cut?

The English Secondary National Curriculum sets out three aims: they are that children should become:

- Successful learners
- Confident individuals
- Responsible citizens

The English Primary National Curriculum has no such corresponding aims (although they were nearly introduced as part of the 2010 'Rose Review', a revision of the primary curriculum that was not implemented after a change of government), so most primary schools have their own aims proudly emblazoned in the foyer and set out in their website and brochure.

The importance of aims and the way they should influence the curriculum was stressed in the *Cambridge Primary Review* ('Children, their world, their education' Alexander et al. 2009). This set out 12 aims that should drive primary education itself and not just the curriculum. The *Cambridge Review* pointed out that schools themselves could take up these aims and it was not necessary to wait for the government to do so. The question is how much these school aims impact upon the curriculum, or whether they get subverted by national considerations.

One of those considerations is the Attainment Targets within the English National Curriculum; one for each subject, set out in eight helpful levels. (There is a descriptor for each level that set out the expected attainment for that level. The levels do not relate directly to year groups or age, but there is an expectation that children will have attained Level 2 by the age of 7, and Level 4 by the age of 11. Some children at these ages will attain Levels 3 or 5.)

So, surely these Attainment Targets tell us what we are trying to achieve? They are targets, after all. In English primary schools, they tend to mean that we are trying to get as many children as we possibly can up to Level 5. For some schools, it is a matter of Level 5 in English or Maths only, so the influence on 'what we are trying to achieve' is not just the Attainment Targets themselves, but the way people put more value on some of them than others. This might come from League Tables, School Improvement Partners (SIPs) and Ofsted Inspections.

But is the attaining of Level 5, even in a wide range of subjects, a sufficient aspiration in itself? Attaining Level 5 might go some way to achieving the first of the three secondary National Curriculum aims, but what about the other two? And what about our school's aims? And do we have to choose? Could we have both Level 5 *and* wider aims? Are overall aims and Attainment Targets at all reconcilable?

This book will argue that it is not a matter of 'either . . . or'. We do not have to choose between Noble Aims or Attainment Targets. In fact, it is when we take account of our aims and use them as a basis for design that the curriculum starts to fall into place, and so does children's learning.

The three circles

The American business guru, Simon Sinek, talks about building successful companies. You can see his 'TED' talk on www.ted.com/simonsinek. In this talk, he shows three concentric circles labelled Why?, How? and What?. 'Why?' is at the centre (see Figure 1.2). Sinek argues that most companies spend their time focusing on what it is that they produce, and a little time thinking about how their product is different from and better than their rival's. Few ask themselves why they are in business at all. He suggests that really successful companies like Apple draw their success from starting with the 'Why'. In Apple's case it is to make information and communication technology easy to use, attractive and intuitive, supportive of what CEO Steve Jobs calls the 'Liberal Arts'. Apple then ask *how* they can do that: by making simple devices that are good to look at and hold, that have very few buttons and run software that doesn't need a huge instruction book to use.

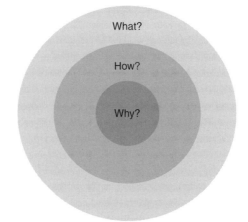

Figure 1.2 The three circles

That brings them to *what* they should produce: ipods, iphones and ipads. The 'What' is really good because they started with the 'Why'.

Sinek extends his analysis to really successful communicators and movements. He talks about figures such as Martin Luther King who had a really strong 'Why'. King didn't start with the 'What' and so decided to organise protests and sit-ins and make speeches, and then wonder *how* he could organise them and *why* he needed demonstrations anyway. He started with the 'Why' and everything else fell into place. Half a million people turned up in Washington on one day in March 1968, even though the event was never advertised and no one had Facebook. Sinek points out that Martin Luther King had a dream, not a business plan.

Sinek also argues that the answer to the commercial 'Why?' is not: 'To make money'. This is essential to an understanding of this analysis. He suggests that making money is the *outcome* of getting all the other bits right, and that companies that start only with a desire to make money and then wonder what they can do to make it, seldom succeed. If the main driver for an organisation is to make money, then product quality and customer satisfaction are compromised and the company is less successful. The ipod and iphone are really successful because they spring from the ideal of beautiful, intuitive technology. This drives the product design; the designers, not the accountants, are in charge; and as a result the accountants are happy.

Sinek does not apply his analysis to schools and the curriculum, but the comparison is clear to see. When you think about it, most curriculum planning in schools is about the 'What?' We spend our time thinking about *what* it is we want the children to learn. We are in the outer circle. Planning meetings are often about taking the programmes of study and organising them into programmes and lessons to answer the questions, 'What have we got to cover?' and 'What are we going to teach?' Then we spend a bit of time thinking about *how* we are going to teach the 'what'. But we seldom get to the '*Why*' which is at the centre of things. Why do we want them to learn these things in the first place?

And Sinek's key point also applies to education. Level 5 or A* at GCSE is not the 'Why?' in education, but if we get the curriculum right, then such success will be the outcome. In fact, a school is much more likely to be successful in terms of the Level 5s if it starts with the 'Why?' Ofsted has good evidence of this in England in their Ofsted Report *Twenty Outstanding Primary Schools* ref. 090170 (2009).

Curriculum Planning is all about arranging the 'What' in the outer circle. Curriculum Design is about starting from the inner circle, and arriving at the 'What' by considering the 'How'. It is through the process of curriculum design that we shall arrive at a world-class curriculum that enables children to explore the world and find their place within it.

The Fruit Machine

It is because the school in the example is clear about the 'Why' that it is able to accommodate the Fruit Machine, and does not worry about whether the time children spend on it will detract from the curriculum. The school sees it as part of the curriculum, and can see how the experience can include learning in key aspects of the programmes. The spreadsheets are part of ICT, the budgeting part of maths, the sourcing and health aspects are part of science. You can see the implications across the curriculum without needing to list them here. The teacher used lessons to help children acquire the knowledge and develop the skills and understanding that they needed in order to run the Fruit Machine. This is what lessons are for. But the learning was powerful because the children had a motivation to learn the things they needed and could see the point; they also had a real and practical context in which they could immediately apply their new learning; and they had a huge emotional commitment. All of this makes learning exciting, engaging and real.

These lessons were not planned long in advance because the setting up of the Fruit Machine came spontaneously from the children themselves. The teacher did not know it was going to happen. The school was able to respond to this because its planning system is around the 'Why' and 'How', rather than being focused on the 'What'. This system gives the teachers the flexibility to draw upon the elements of the 'What' within developing situations. They are confident to be flexible and take advantage of rich learning situations, because they are clear about their aims and have a system to ensure that the flexible curriculum will be coherent and balanced overall. We shall look at this system in detail in Chapter 9.

Letting the Fruit Machine continue to develop enabled the experience to become richer and richer. At one point, the children decided that if they grew carrots (a popular line at morning break) in the school garden they could increase their profit. But first, some profit needed to be ploughed (literally) back into planting seeds. It was when they decided that they should also plant some apple trees that some serious discussion took place. 'Apple trees take years before they produce fruit, and we shall all have left the school by then, so won't get any profit,' some said. 'But if we don't plant some, there never will be apple trees for the next generation,' replied others.

We often talk to children about citizenship, but it is not easy to put them into a situation where they are able to make real-life decisions for the greater good, and experience this aspect of citizenship first hand. The richness of learning is in the experience itself, but is brought out by the teacher's confidence to allow it to develop. The confidence comes from a system that is not all about arranging 'content', but is about the deeper goals.

More than the first chapter

This first chapter has attempted to put the curriculum into a wider context. It is more than the National Curriculum and involves more than lessons, subjects and knowledge (although it involves all of those). It is about key aims and a system of design that is more than curriculum planning. It is about the set of experiences that children need in order to learn the things we want them to learn to equip them for the journey of life. If we want them to learn knowledge, skills and understanding as well as to develop personally, emotionally, socially and morally as human beings, then that set of experiences needs to be rich and varied.

The Fruit Machine was an example of rich learning that involved skills and understanding as well as knowledge; that enabled children to develop personal and social skills and to engage as citizens. It is an example of learning beyond the National Curriculum, learning beyond lessons, beyond subjects and beyond knowledge. Not all learning can be like that, but when some learning is like that, it can impact across the curriculum, and take it beyond the ordinary. It can take children beyond the ordinary and start to open up the world for them.

We now go beyond the first chapter, and open up the rest of the book to look in more detail at what would take a curriculum beyond the ordinary.

In case you hadn't worked it out, the three design questions are:

- What are we trying to achieve?
- How should we organise learning most effectively to achieve those things?
- How will we know if we have been successful?

2

A 21st century curriculum?

The Radio Station

'May I ask you why you are visiting our school to-day?' The microphone is held by a Year 5 pupil who in her other hand holds a list of visitors and a sheath of questions. This is not the usual welcome to a primary school, but is par for the course in a school with its own radio station. A room has been set up with the slit window and array of equipment usually associated with a professional station. The reporter downloads her interview into a computer and a colleague edits it on screen. She does this without listening but by watching a pulsing line on the screen. Where the line becomes flat she draws a box around this section with the mouse, and deletes it. 'That is just some hesitation, so I'm taking it out.'

On the wall is a list of music, interviews and other pieces, all timed to the second. These are the programmes that will be broadcast to the school during the lunchbreak. Reporters scour the school and surrounding area for stories. Pupils perform their own music as well as play their favourites. They write and perform plays and produce comedy programmes and quizzes. There are interactive programmes with listeners texting in their thoughts. The programmes go out at every break every day.

Reversing the roles, the Year 5 interviewer was asked how she had time for the interview and why she did not need to be in a lesson. 'I have to negotiate that with my teacher. I knew you were coming at 10 a.m. so I arranged to leave the English lesson for ten minutes. My friend will help me catch up on what I've missed. We all take it in turn so none of us miss much, and we all help each other. We've all had to apply for these jobs and be interviewed, and everyone listens to the programmes, so it's all worthwhile. We are really pleased if one of our reports gets broadcast – they only choose the best.'

> At break, the pupils congregate around the speakers in the recreation areas, keen to listen. The radio station is an integral part of school life – and an integral part of learning.
>
> Anyone who had been in this inner city school three years earlier would have been amazed by this scene. The school was then in 'special measures' with behaviour 'out of hand'. Engaging children actively in their learning, making learning exciting and relevant, and giving children purpose and some independence transformed the school in terms of behaviour and attainment.

Here we are in the second decade of the 21st century and people are still wondering if we have a curriculum that fully prepares our young people to live successfully in it. People are asking this question all around the world, and some countries are taking particular steps to ensure that their curricula respond to new challenges.

(You may be wondering why a chapter about a 21st century curriculum would start with a story about a radio station – radio doesn't sound very 21st century, does it? Read on and all will be revealed.)

In England, the question about a 21st century curriculum is particularly pertinent. The review of the whole National Curriculum announced in 2011 is based on the premise that 'We intend to restore the National Curriculum to its original purpose – a minimum national entitlement for all our young people organised around the subject disciplines.' These subject disciplines

Table 2.1 Spotting the difference

1905	1989
Reading and writing	English
Arithmetic	Mathematics
Nature study	Science
History	History
Geography	Geography
Drawing	Art
Physical exercise	Physical Education
Singing	Music
Manual training	Design and Technology
Housewifery	Information Technology

around which the curriculum is to be organised for the 21st century bear a remarkable similarity to the National Curriculum set out by the 'Revised Code' of 1905, as shown in Table 2.1.

Can you spot the difference? No prizes for this one: The names have changed, but beyond that, Information Technology is in, and Housewifery is out. There are, no doubt, some people who regret the omission of housewifery.

The world that young people entered on leaving school in 1905 was very different from now. In England, they came out into a fairly static Edwardian society where they worked in occupations such as agriculture, manufacturing, mining, commerce or administration – or they became housewives – and expected to do the same job in pretty much the same way for the rest of their lives. The curriculum of that time was calculated to prepare them for that static sort of world.

The second decade of the 21st century is a very different place, and in particular it is very much less static. It is expected that people will change jobs several times in their working life, and not just from one employer to another, but taking on fundamentally different occupations. It is predicted that in 25 years' time over half the jobs people will be doing have not yet been invented. And, of course, many young people will struggle to find jobs at all. How do we prepare our young people for such a world? This is not to suggest that education is only there to prepare young people for employment; the changes and challenges are widespread and affect all aspects of personal life as well.

It is not necessary to labour this point here. We all know the recent extraordinary rate of technological change and the impact this has on employment and on society in general. We could add to that such factors as globalisation, the changing balance of economic and political power from the West to the East, changing social and economic patterns, climate change. The impact is not just on employment, it is also on social patterns and private life. Who would have thought 20 years ago that the seemingly major form of social interaction between young people is through a hand-held electronic device?

So, if the 21st century is so different from 1905, will the same set of subjects suffice to prepare our young people for the life ahead of them? If we need something different, what is it: a different set of subjects, changes within the subjects? Or is it something else?

What do young people need to learn in order to succeed in the 21st century?

When the former Qualifications Curriculum Authority (QCA) started the review of the English Secondary and then the Primary Curriculum in 2005, it asked a wide range of people this very question. It asked parents, teachers, governors, employers, faith groups, the wider public and pupils themselves.

In all these groups, all over the country, from diverse backgrounds from the Confederation of British Industry to local parish councillors, the list was remarkably similar.

Young people need to:

- Be creative
- Communicate well
- Be literate and numerate
- Solve problems
- Work together in teams
- Have a global perspective
- Show initiative
- Work independently
- Be a life-long learner

Do you agree with that list? What would you add, or take away? Are there any surprises?

It is interesting that in all those different groups surveyed by the QCA in England, nobody said that what young people really needed was 5A*-C passes at GCSE, or Level 5 in the Year 6 SAT. Everyone listed wider skills, attitudes and dispositions that they saw as equipping a young person for the future. It is also interesting that nobody mentioned subjects either. Yet it is the subjects that form the basis of most of what goes on in schools and are the statutory basis of the English National Curriculum. Perhaps everyone took the subjects for granted so didn't bother to list them. Perhaps the questions were 'loaded' encouraging people to be thinking of higher or wider aspirations. Or perhaps people saw the things on the list as more important than subjects. Perhaps we do not have to choose between high attainment in subjects and wider aims.

Whatever the reason, meeting after meeting and group after group came up with similar lists that go beyond subjects. And most of the things on the list above are very similar to Singapore's '21st Century Competencies'.

In an effort to focus on this impact, the QCA conducted its wide consultations by asking people to draw a successful learner, and then write around the picture the factors for success in the 21st century. People were invited to look at their list and ask: Which of the things on the list are skills, which are knowledge, and which are qualities? Lines were then drawn linking knowledge to the brain, skills to the hand and qualities to the heart. This may not be anatomically correct, but it presents a strong visual image. In almost every case, most of the things people wanted children to learn led to the heart. Yet most of the planned curriculum is to do with the brain.

It is a useful exercise to carry out within a school with staff or with governors and parents. It not only promotes discussion about some key aims and aspirations, it helps focus on the different nature of learning within a curriculum, and raises questions about what should be the basis of curriculum design.

Common around the world

Interestingly, people's view of what young people need to prepare them for the 21st century seems to be the same all over the world. The same exercise has been repeated in many countries, and the results are very similar. The first picture in Figure 2.1 was drawn in Leeds, and you will no doubt recognise the language in the second picture and so will see that people in Lithuania say exactly the same.

In almost all cases, people respond to their perceptions of the changing world of the 21st century. This is why they rate the importance of such attributes as confidence, flexibility and resilience (darbstus and smalsus). They also recognise that successful young people will need to be active rather than passive, so we see the need to be enthusiastic, brave, risk-takers, and investigators (drasus and linksmas). There is a worldwide recognition that individualism will not be a sufficient quality for the 21st century, and that co-operation and team work will be necessary. Other common features across the world are creativity, communication, problem-solving and critical thinking.

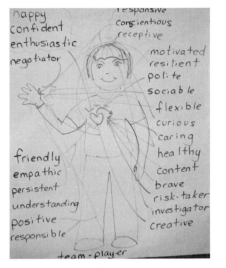

Figure 2.1 A successful learner

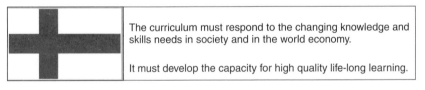

	The curriculum must respond to the changing knowledge and skills needs in society and in the world economy. It must develop the capacity for high quality life-long learning.

Figure 2.2 Finland

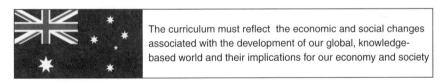

	The curriculum must reflect the economic and social changes associated with the development of our global, knowledge-based world and their implications for our economy and society

Figure 2.3 Victoria

Taking account of wider challenges

Many countries around the world recognise the wider challenges of the 21st century and have sought to build these into their national curricula. For example, what Finland (a country that features near the top of most international comparisons) says is shown in Figure 2.2.

What Victoria, Australia, says is described in Figure 2.3.

So how are countries 'reflecting the economic and social changes' in their curricula?

Almost every country that has revised its national curriculum recently has added a range of skills and competencies along with aspects of personal development that we looked at in Chapter 1. They see these as augmenting the subject areas and adding a new dimension to these areas and to learning overall. We have already mentioned the two sets of competencies in the Singapore curriculum, which are listed in Figure 2.4.

Singapore		
	Social and emotional competencies	21st century competencies
	• Self-awareness • Self-management • Social awareness • Relationship management • Responsible decision making	• Civic literacy, • Global awareness • Cross-curricular skills • Critical and media skills • Information and communication skills

Figure 2.4 Singapore competencies

New Zealand also has a set of 'Key Competencies' that will operate across the curriculum, as displayed in Figure 2.5.

New Zealand	
	Key competencies
	• Thinking • Using languages, symbols and texts • Managing self • Relating to others

Figure 2.5 New Zealand Competencies

The United Nations Educational, Scientific and Cultural Organisation (UNESCO) in 2009 identified four '21st Century Competencies' (Ananiadoui & Claro 2009), and recommended them to member nations as needing to underpin all curricula. These competencies are the 'four C's' of:

- Communication
- Critical thinking and problem-solving

- Collaboration

- Creativity

UNESCO helped to develop a national curriculum for the new nation of Kosovo, and six different sorts of competencies have been identified within that curriculum, as detailed in Figure 2.6.

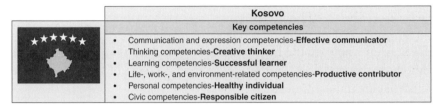

Kosovo
Key competencies
• Communication and expression competencies-**Effective communicator** • Thinking competencies-**Creative thinker** • Learning competencies-**Successful learner** • Life-, work-, and environment-related competencies-**Productive contributor** • Personal competencies-**Healthy individual** • Civic competencies-**Responsible citizen**

Figure 2.6 Kosovo competencies

And what about England?

You might be wondering at this point where the English Primary National Curriculum fits in with this. The 'Key Skills' and 'Thinking Skills' that we mentioned in Chapter 1 (the one that you could list without having to look them up!) were added to the National Curriculum in 2000, so were ready for the 21st century, as expressed in Figure 2.7.

England (Primary)	
Key Skills	**Thinking skills**
• Communication • Application of number • Information technology • Working with others • Improving own learning and performance • Problem solving	• Information processing • Reasoning • Inquiry • Creative thinking • Evaluation

Figure 2.7 England – Primary skills

When the English Secondary National Curriculum was revised in 2008, a set of 'Personal, Learning and Thinking Skills' (PLTS) was added. Many English primary schools are using these PLTS instead of the Key and Thinking Skills of the Primary Curriculum, even though the latter are statutory for primary schools and the PLTS are not statutory at all. The PLTS are listed in Figure 2.8.

England (Secondary)		
	Personal, Learning and Thinking Skills	
	• Independent enquirers • Effective participants • Reflective learners • Team workers • Self-managers • Creative thinkers	

Figure 2.8 England – Secondary skills

When you compare the English lists, you see that as well as being more comprehensive and specific there are three elements of the Primary Key Skills that are quite different from any of the PLTS:

• Communication

• Application of number

• Information technology.

These are significant to curriculum design because they are aspects of subjects (English, Maths and ICT), unlike the more general skills such as 'thinking' or 'decision making' which are skills that are not located within one subject area. However, they are listed separately because they are aspects of those subjects that apply to all the other subjects as well and this gives them a special status. They also go beyond being skills because each of them requires a considerable amount of knowledge and understanding as well, so they are really 'competencies'.

The Rose Review also included these three elements when it set out its 'Essentials for Learning and Life' and called them, for want of a more snappy title, 'Essential literacy, numeracy and ICT'. These are listed in Figure 2.9.

Essential literacy, numeracy and ICT are basically the 'communication, application of number and information technology' skills of the existing primary Key Skills. They are also present in one form or another in almost every revised curriculum around the world, and they are of key importance to a primary school curriculum in the 21st century. We shall return to them below.

The Rose Proposals		
	Essentials for Learning and Life	
	• Essential Literacy, Numeracy & ICT • Learning and thinking skills • Personal and emotional skills • Social skills	

Figure 2.9 'Essentials for Learning and Life'

A response to the 21st century

As we look at other countries, we see that they are responding the challenges of the present century by adding a range of skills and competencies, and aspects of personal development to their national curricula. This does not mean that they have abandoned subjects, or that they do not see them as important, but that they see the need for the curriculum to go beyond them in order to enable young people to cope with life in the 21st century. There is a widespread recognition that the learning contained within the set of subjects that may have served people well in 1905 will be insufficient to equip people for the world they face a century later.

The rise of computer technology is only one aspect of the change, but is one with a significant impact on learning itself and the way in which we view the world (Heppell et al. 2004). We are still at the beginning of understanding the implications for schools and the curriculum (Facer, Furlong and Sutherland 2003), and the implications for the way in which children's learning is developing (Pahl 2005; Goswami and Bryant 2007).

The range of things added falls into the two categories we considered in Chapter 1: Personal Development and Key Skills. There is also the new category of the 'Essential literacy, numeracy and ICT' discussed above. This is the very equipment that children need in order to explore that new and vast world and to find their place within it.

We will take them one at a time.

Personal development

The QCA consultation on what young people need to equip them for the 21st century listed mainly aspects of personal development rather than elements of knowledge and understanding within the subject domains. The competencies listed by countries revising their national curricula also contain many aspects of personal development. These aspects fall into several categories that have significant implications for curriculum design.

Some elements of personal development are skills. A skill is the ability to perform a physical or mental operation. As such, skills can be learned and can to some extent be taught. They generally need practice through the performance of the skill itself, rather than reading about the skill or listening to someone explaining it. This can be seen in a physical skill such as hitting a ball with a tennis racquet; you can watch any number of demonstrations, but you only learn the skill by hitting the ball yourself. The same is true of mental skills; they have to be performed to be acquired.

Some of the other aspects of personal development on the lists are not skills that can be learned or practised in this way, but are attitudes, values, qualities and dispositions. For example, 'self-confidence' is not a skill than can be taught, but is a quality that is developed through a particular set of experiences (usually those where some success was achieved). To 'show initiative' would be a disposition as it is a tendency to act in a particular way. This tendency may be the result of the possession of certain skills, but is not a skill in itself. To be 'caring' or 'curious' would seem to be more like an attitude.

You may well disagree with specifics here and think, for instance, that 'caring' is a value rather than an attitude. There is not overall consensus in this area; many of these categories overlap and there is no clear agreement on where one ends and another begins. In fact, some people do not see them as categories at all, but as part of a continuum of personal development. However, it is critically important for a curriculum designer to give thought to the sort of experiences that would promote the different aspects of personal development. It is no good expecting children to develop skills without opportunities to practise them, and it is equally pointless expecting children to develop qualities through practice.

This does not mean that the desired attitudes, values, qualities and dispositions or anything else on the continuum cannot be promoted through the curriculum. Indeed, it is important that they should be promoted. But they tend to be the outcome of a long series of experiences rather than things that can be taught discretely like Venn Diagrams or the formation of ox-bow lakes.

If attitudes, values, qualities and disposition are the result of a whole series of experiences then we need to give thought to the totality of the experiences children undergo in our schools. In Chapter 1 we looked at the way in which learning does not just occur in lessons but through such things as the routines of the school, events and through the ethos and relationships that prevail. These are of critical importance to a whole range of personal development, especially the ethos and relationships. These aspects of personal development are long-term and the result of the whole experience each child receives through school. Of course, children are in school for a relatively short proportion of each week and year, and there will be other influences on their personal development, but schools can still be very influential when the experiences are positive.

Within the lists, there are personal skills that do need to be built specifically into the curriculum. These would include working collaboratively, self-management, independent working, managing feelings, adapting behaviour to others and negotiating. Some of these might be seen as personal or emotional skills, and some as social skills. They can be structured directly into the curriculum and improved through practice. We shall consider how best to do this in Chapter 4.

Key skills

Not all the 'Key' and 'Thinking' skills of the English Primary Curriculum are aspects of personal development. Many are skills that relate more to the cognitive domain, and that can be applied across the curriculum. These key skills are sometimes referred to as 'Thinking and Learning Skills', or 'Key Skills' as they are important to learning across the curriculum. They are the cognitive skills that enable children to make sense of all the information they find out about the world. Because these skills apply across all human knowledge, and so across the curriculum, some countries, such as Singapore, refer to them as 'cross curricular skills'. In its co-development work with schools, QCA identified five such skills that tend to occur in most countries and that broadly subsume the rest:

- Investigate
- Analyse and synthesise
- Create and develop
- Evaluate
- Communicate

These are similar to UNESCO's '21st Century Competencies' (Critical thinking, Creativity, Communication and Collaboration) minus the 'social' element of collaboration. They could also be thought of as codifying children's natural impulse to find things out and to make sense of the world (Laevers 1998 and Goswami 2008).

Table 2.2 gives some more detail about each skill. You could use this list or amend it or draw up your own, but most sets will contain these elements somewhere or the other. The name 'Key Skills' is used in this book to refer to these skills that apply across the curriculum.

There is nothing sacrosanct about the list in Table 2.2, and many countries and individual schools work successfully from different lists, but the above five elements do tend to occur widely. The reason why different lists can work equally successfully is that each skill is not discrete anyway, nor can the skills be taught or learned discretely. That is why, when attempts are made to break down the process into discrete elements, there will be disagreements about what the elements are, or where one starts and another

Table 2.2 Five 'Key Skills' identified by the Qualifications Curriculum Authority

Key Skills	
Investigate	Ask relevant questions, identify problems and question assumptions. Make observations, compare and contrast. Collect relevant information in a systematic way.
Analyse and synthesise	Analyse data collected to identify patterns and relationships. Synthesise information to make generalisations.
Create and develop ideas	Use imagination to explore possibilities and generate ideas. Suggest and try out innovative alternatives and find solutions to problems. Make reasoned decisions. Combine a range of approaches to find alternative solutions.
Evaluate	Develop effective criteria for judging effectiveness. Suggest improvements, modify and refine processes and outcomes, and analyse effectiveness in relation to intention. Ensure the practicality of ideas and developments.
Communicate	Communicate with a range of audiences, using and combining a range of media in ways appropriate to the audience and subject.

ends. (The Rose Review in England used this list and then shortened it to four elements by subsuming 'analyse and synthesise' into 'investigate').

Many countries include 'problem solving' and 'critical thinking' in their list, while other countries see these as the result of all the others. (To solve a problem, you need to investigate, analyse and synthesise the information, create and develop different solutions and evaluate possible solutions. Critical thinking involves investigation, analysis, synthesis and evaluation.) What is important in curriculum design is to be aware of the importance of a set of key skills within and across the subject areas, and to build these into the curriculum.

These five skills can be seen as a common process of thinking and learning that is applied across the areas of learning. Listing them separately does not mean that they exist in isolation one from another; they are usually deployed and developed in concert. The line between the elements is often blurred; for example, analysis and synthesis could well be seen as part of investigating as it would be hard to do the one without the other. For example, children who wanted to make a wild life pond in the school grounds would investigate by finding out what lived in an existing pond nearby, analyse by distinguishing the different types, synthesise by sorting them into groups (plants and animals or fish, insects and crustaceans etc.), create and develop by producing their own pond designs, evaluate by checking that these would actually work and then communicate their ideas by drawings and plans. As far as the children are concerned, it is one seamless process. The holistic nature of this learning is recognised by academics as well as children (Gardner 1999; Perkins, Bonnet and Miyani 2005; and Goswami & Bryant 2007).

Essential literacy, numeracy and ICT: back to basics!

A curriculum for primary schools must ensure that children learn certain basic skills of literacy and numeracy. These take time to acquire, but lie at the heart of all other learning. They unlock learning in other areas, and allow young people to operate effectively in their lives. This is no less true in the 21st century than it was in the 20th, although the emphasis has changed, the contexts in which the skills are applied are much wider, and the range of skills itself is now more extensive. It would also be difficult to live and learn in the 21st century without basic skills in information technology.

The old 19th and 20th century 'basics' are not sufficient for the 21st century. There still are some 'basics' that every child needs to learn, but they are not the same ones. The world has moved on.

This is reflected across the world where countries now identify these skills separately from the subjects. This is seen in different forms, such as 'Civic Literacy' and 'ICT' in Singapore and 'Using languages, symbols and texts' in New Zealand. The Rose Review in England also saw 'essential literacy, numeracy and ICT' as distinct from the study of English, Mathematics and ICT where concepts and ideas might be studied for their own sake as well as for their functionality.

The 'essentialness' comes from the need to use these skills in contexts other than the subjects in which they are normally located. For example, you need to be able to read in order to access learning in almost any other subject, and in order to function as a 21st century citizen. Similarly, you need to be able to speak and to understand what other people are saying to you. You need a level of numeracy in order to access other subjects too. Everything from Science to PE has an element of number, measurement, data handling and shape. It would also be difficult to function adequately as a citizen without a minimum level of numeracy. And it has become as essential to have a level of competence in information technology. What makes these essential is their functionality. They enable you to learn other things, and are essential to be able to function competently in the 21st century.

These 'essential' or 'functional' aspects are really competencies rather than skills, because to operate effectively they require a certain amount of knowledge and understanding as well as skill. To be fully effective, the learner also needs the appropriate attitudes and dispositions. This combination is a competency.

The identification of 'essential' elements leaves other aspects of English, Maths and ICT that are, therefore, not seen as essential in the same way. This seems an odd notion at first. When you take out the functional communication element from English, what do you have left? Mainly the creative and literary aspects: poetry, drama, novels, creative writing, stories, Shakespeare, Austen, Dhal, Rowling.

All of these are important, but are not *essential* in order to function as a citizen or to learn geography or science. Appreciating Beethoven's music is also important, and equally not essential in the functional way that aspects of reading and calculating are. The music and poetry enhance life and are an important part of any curriculum, but their place within it is different from the 'essential' elements of literacy, numeracy and ICT, because of their relationship to other learning.

The reason that English and maths are seen as more important than other subjects, and so the focus of high-stakes public testing, is because of their functionality in communication, comprehension and calculation. Yet, because *part* of these subjects is essential, somehow or other, *all* of the subjects is seen as essential. The result is that we test children on their ability to appreciate Shakespeare, and if they are unable to do so, we say that they can't read. The same is true of Maths and ICT. There is a distinction between being able to use ICT effectively, and the study of ICT as a subject that would enable you eventually to write computer programs.

Newspapers and some politicians in England are often urging schools to 'get back to basics'. By that they mean a focus on what used to be referred to as the 'Three Rs' of reading, writing and arithmetic (obviously, spelling was not a strong point in those days). They were certainly the key skills for 1905, but the 21st century is making different demands. The range of communication is now much wider altogether. There was no demand for ICT skills in 1905, but they have now become essential. The range of mathematics commonly demanded is also wider than the simple arithmetic that was sufficient in 1905.

It could, therefore, be argued that what we need is no longer the 'Three Rs' of 'reading, writing and arithmetic', but the '3 Cs' of communication, calculation and computer competence. (You may point out that this neat name doesn't work because essential numeracy is wider than calculation, and ICT is more than computers – however, it is much neater if they all start with 'C'. There is good precedent for taking such liberties – neither writing nor arithmetic starts with 'R'! So, let's stick with 3Cs.)

The 3 Cs

There will always be disagreements about what should be in, and what should be out, of any sort of list of this kind, but the identification of essential basic elements is an important element in curriculum design. If we remember Sinek's 'Why', it will be helpful to us. The reason we are equipping children with these 3Cs is to help them navigate their voyage of discovery through life. This should be our touchstone. 'How' we do that is by helping them develop

Table 2.3 The 3C competencies

Communication	Calculation	Computer competency
Listen attentively, talk clearly and confidently about their thoughts, opinions and ideas, listening carefully to others so that they can refine their thinking and express themselves effectively. Read accurately and fluently to comprehend and critically respond to texts of all kinds, on paper and on screen, in order to access ideas and information. Write, present and broadcast a range of ideas in a variety of forms for a range of audiences and purposes; communicate ideas accurately on paper, on screen and through multimodal texts. Analyse, evaluate and criticise a range of language to draw out meaning, purpose and effect.	Represent and model situations using a range of tools and applying logic and reasoning in order to predict, plan and try out options. Use numbers and measurement for accurate calculation, understanding of scale and make reasonable estimates. Interpret and interrogate mathematical data in graphs, spreadsheets and diagrams in order to draw inferences, recognise patterns and trends and assess likelihood. Justify and support decisions and proposals, communicating accurately using maths language, symbols and diagrams.	Find and select information from digital and online sources. Create, manipulate and process information using technology to capture and organise data, investigate patterns, explore options; combine still and moving images, sounds and texts to create multimedia products. Collaborate, communicate and share information using connectivity to work with and present to people and audiences within and beyond the school. Refine and improve their work; make full use of the nature and pliability of digital information to explore options and improve outcomes.

key skills and competencies. 'What' these key skills and competencies are becomes much clearer when we remember 'Why' we are doing this at all.

The list in Table 2.3 is similar to the one in the Rose Review, and those of other countries. How does it measure up to that basic 'Why'? If children could do these things, would it help them explore the world and find their place within it?

You may agree with this list, or wish to amend or refine it. Many schools are finding it a useful starting point in identifying key aspects of learning which are essential in the 21st century. The list is reasonably up to date with its mention of digital media within literacy, but some schools have gone farther than this. The important, and helpful, point is to identify a range of access skills that can be built into a wide range of experiences.

The importance of identifying these '3 Cs' or essential elements of literacy, numeracy and ICT, is the way they then fit within curriculum design. If they are so important, do we allocate most of our time to these and then fit everything else in afterwards? Or is there a better way?

The school radio station

If you can remember the beginning of this chapter, you might, of course, be wanting to suggest that a radio station sounds particularly 20th century and is therefore an odd illustration of a 21st century curriculum. Why don't they have a television station if they want to be up to date? Why don't they have streamed video or a continuous blog? Have they not heard of the internet? Actually, they have all of these, and the programmes are available as podcasts as well. It is just that the radio station is a really good place to start learning how to create in different media. It also illustrates the point that it is not just a matter of having the latest technology; what is much more important is how that technology is used. In this case it is used to give children independence and to release creativity, to approach subjects from a different angle, and to build a range of skills and competencies.

It also is an interesting illustration of subjects within the curriculum. The amount of learning involved in running the station involves a whole range of subjects: reading, writing, speaking, listening, maths, science, ICT, music, drama and citizenship. But none of these appears as a separate subject. As soon as the subjects are applied in life they begin to lose their boundaries.

The radio station is also contributing to children's personal development, social and negotiating skills. Just think how many of the '3 Cs' and the four UNESCO 'Key Competencies' are integrally involved in running the radio station: communication, collaboration, critical thinking and creativity, calculation and computer competence (how many more 'Cs' could you get?).

Radio might be 'old-tech', but the competencies developed by the children are truly 21st century.

The next chapter of this book will look at how the personal development, skills and competencies can fit with the subjects or disciplines to create rich learning for children.

3

A framework for the curriculum

There's Something at the Bottom of the Garden

Year 1 were making a vegetable garden and by way of preparation visited the local allotments to see what grew there. Before the visit, they had discussed the sort of plants that they might see and the questions they might ask the allotment holders who had agreed to show them round. There was a degree of excitement as they walked up the muddy tracks between the rows of cabbages, peas and beans. 'These are the things we were talking about!'

Unfortunately, their attention began to wane as the allotment holder was showing them the beans, even thought she urged the children to pick their own and taste them. They had seen the compost heap in the corner and wanted to know what it was. As it happened, the allotment holder was even more enthusiastic about the compost heap than she was about her vegetables, and was soon taking off the successive layers and showing the children the process of rotting down.

Why is it that some things catch children's imaginations? If you had planned to get them excited by taking them to a compost heap it would never have worked at all. As it was, the compost heap was the star of the show, and thing they had to have in the Year 1 garden.

With the help of allotment holders, compost heaps were installed and the school's vegetable waste was no longer wasted. The heaps became the focus of much scientific investigation. Experiments were carried out on rotting in different conditions: shade, light, damp, dry, heat and cold, and the results were examined closely. The children fully appreciated the importance of compost to the growth of plants.

The relationship between allotment holder and children became strong and much contact was made out of school hours. The children became keen gardeners and eventually were able to cook and eat their own produce. But whenever they showed visitors round their garden, they never forgot that great source of pride as well as growth: the Year 1 compost heap.

It is all very well to talk about the lofty aims for the curriculum in Chapter 1, and then add lists of skills, competencies and personal development in Chapter 2. But, how do all these elements come together along with the subject areas to provide a coherent curriculum for young people? How do lofty aspirations impact on the curriculum of a primary school? What difference do they make to what Year 3 will be doing on Thursday afternoon? If they do not impact on what actually goes on, then they will remain lofty aspirations and nothing more.

What these other countries have done is to create curriculum frameworks that provide a structure that shows how all the elements can come together to impact on learning. This is often done by establishing some key principles and values that need to underpin the whole curriculum, and then identifying the key skills and competencies that run right across it. This, in itself, is still theoretical and 'words on paper', but we need to follow this through to see how it impacts on curriculum design and so on the children themselves.

Singapore has a set of 'Desired Outcomes' and 'Principles' that provide a setting for the competencies, as tabulated in Figure 3.1.

Singapore			
Desired Outcomes	**Principles**	**Social and Emotional Competencies**	**21st Century Competencies**
 • Confident person • Self-directed learner • Active contributor • Concerned citizen	• Flexibility and diversity • Broad-based holistic education • Teach less–learn more	• Self-awareness • Self-management • Social awareness • Relationship management • Responsible decision making	• Civic literacy, • Global awareness • Cross-curricular skills • Critical and media skills • Information and communication skills

Figure 3.1 Singapore framework

New Zealand		
Principles	**Values**	**Key Competencies**
 • High expectations • Treat of Waitangi • Cultural diversity • Inclusion • Learning to learn • Community engagement • Coherence • Future focus	• Excellence • Innovation, inquiry and curiosity • Diversity • Equity • Community participation • Ecological sustainability • Integrity • Respect	• Thinking • Using languages, symbols and texts • Managing self • Relating to others

Figure 3.2 New Zealand framework

New Zealand has a framework of Principles, Values and Key Competencies, which are detailed in Figure 3.2.

Does England have a curriculum framework?

The National Curriculum for Primary Schools in England has been put together more piecemeal since 1989. It started off as a set of subjects for which there were 'Programmes of Study' and 'Attainment Targets'. In the 1999 revision, an Introduction was added to the Curriculum Handbook setting out 'Values and purposes', 'Aims' and a 'National Framework'. These are commonly referred to as 'the white pages', and most teachers flick past them to get to the subjects. However, they do set out the sort of framework seen in other countries, which is displayed in Figure 3.3.

England			
Aims	**Main Purposes**	**Key Skills**	**Thinking skills**
 • Provide opportunities for all pupils to learn and succeed • Promote pupils' spiritual, moral, social and cultural development and prepare them for the opportunities, responsibilities and experiences of life	• Establish an entitlement • Establish standards • Promote continuity and coherence • Promote public understanding	• Communication • Application of number • Information technology • Working with others • Improving own learning and performance • Problem solving	• Information processing • Reasoning • Inquiry • Creative thinking • Evaluation

Figure 3.3 England framework

The issue in England is that the framework has never been set out as such (have you ever seen that table before?), nor has any overall model been widely propagated that shows how this framework is supposed to impact on the subjects and so influence curriculum design. The reality is that the framework was 'retro-fitted' after the subject programmes had been set out, so was never incorporated properly. The issue is that it doesn't really work as a framework anyway, because it does not provide a model of how the different elements fit together.

A curriculum model

Singapore has set its competencies within a clear framework of outcomes and values, as presented in Figure 3.4.

This stresses the centrality of the competencies but does not show precisely how they fit with the subject areas that are also a requirement of the national curriculum. The Singapore Primary Curriculum model sets the competencies in the context of the subject areas. There are two sets of central skills: Life Skills and Knowledge Skills. The former are broadly to do with personal development, health and well-being, and the latter are the 'key skills' or 'thinking and learning skills'. The subjects areas are grouped into three broad domains, and the skills are shown at the heart of the Curriculum, as seen in Figure 3.5.

In this Framework, physical education is seen as an aspect of 'Life Skills' rather than as a subject. Essential elements of literacy, numeracy and ICT (the 3Cs) are part of 'Knowledge Skills'. The model illustrates the way that the skills impact right across the subject areas, and are central to the curriculum.

The state of Victoria in Australia has a third 'strand' to its curriculum which it calls 'Inter-disciplinary learning'. This is similar to the cross-curricular elements required in Finland and elsewhere, where children are required to engage in thematic studies that join subjects together. The Victoria model sees the three strands inter-weaving rather like a triple helix of DNA, as can be observed in Figure 3.6. It is envisaged that learning experiences are designed to combine these three elements, and we shall look closer at this in the next Chapter.

A more generic model of how all these things fit together shows how the elements of aims, values, subject areas and what we might call '21st century

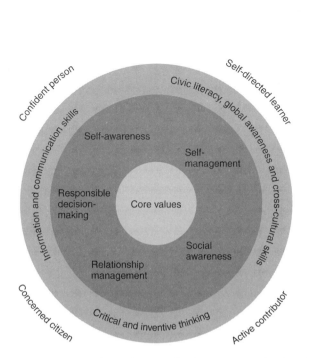

Figure 3.4 Competencies set within a framework of outcomes and values by Singapore

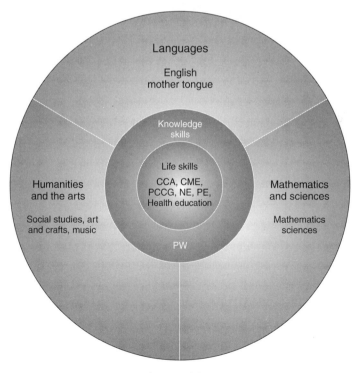

Figure 3.5 Singapore Primary Curriculam model

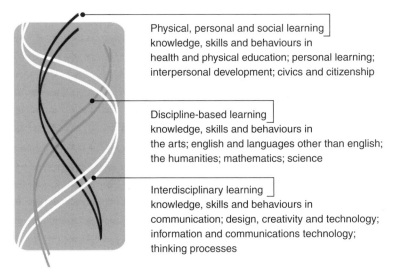

Physical, personal and social learning
knowledge, skills and behaviours in
health and physical education; personal learning;
interpersonal development; civics and citizenship

Discipline-based learning
knowledge, skills and behaviours in
the arts; english and languages other than english;
the humanities; mathematics; science

Interdisciplinary learning
knowledge, skills and behaviours in
communication; design, creativity and technology;
information and communications technology;
thinking processes

Figure 3.6 Victoria Primary Curriculum model

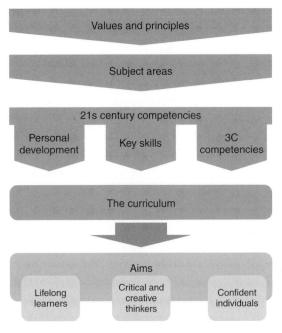

Figure 3.7 A generic model

competencies' fit together to contribute to the whole curriculum, as seen in Figure 3.7. In this model, the values, subjects areas and '21st century competencies' all come together to create the curriculum. And if the curriculum is successful, then it will achieve its ends and young people will develop into lifelong learners, critical thinkers and confident individuals (or whatever aims you have set).

It may seem odd to put the aims at the end in this way. Don't we start from the aims? In terms of design, we do start with the aims, but they should also be the outcome of the curriculum and the measure of its success.

Impact in the classroom

We could also look at the impact another way with the subject areas and the three elements of the competencies contributing to the experiences of the primary curriculum we looked at in Chapter 1 (see Figure 3.8).

Each of the four curriculum elements would be drawn upon to design each of the wide range of learning experiences that children enjoy in school (see Figure 3.9).

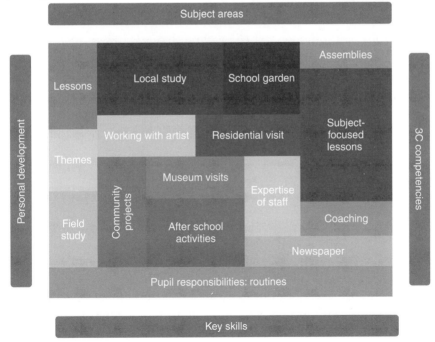

Figure 3.8 Impact in the classroom (1)

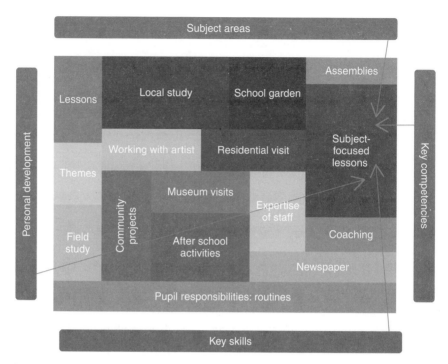

Figure 3.9 Impact in the classroom (2)

In the process of design, the curriculum designer draws upon the four elements to construct the learning experience. But from the point of view of the child, it is the experience that contributes to their learning in the four elements. So, from the child's point of view, the arrows should be the other way round. There is more of this in Chapter 9.

Everything in the garden

When you think of the compost heap, this was an experience in several of the boxes. The school garden is there, but it also impacted on science lessons, and tending the garden also becomes a routine. When we look at the four outside elements, there was a major contribution to science in terms of the growth of plants. There was also a great contribution to personal development in terms of the relationship with older people and the appreciation of the pride that the allotment holders had in their work and plots. Children worked together in teams in the garden and appreciated the contribution each made. There was contribution to the 3C Competencies in the measurements and counting, the writing of emails to the allotment holders and the looking up of information about compost on the web.

Rich experiences like this have no diffulty in making contributions to a wide range of learning. The trick is to recognise the extent of the learning going on, and then to build on it. An effective framework helps us take account of the richness.

And what if my country does not have one of the clear frameworks described above?

Some schools would be delighted to have the opportunity to draw up their own framework, and would relish the task of constructing one. Other schools may think that a framework like Singapore's looks pretty good and could be adapted to cooler climates. Or you may like to make use of the one above. The key is to take the learning you intend for the pupils in your school and think through how it all fits together. Is there any direct way in which your school aims can impact each time a learning experience is designed. What about children's personal development? Is this taken into account when learning is designed? What about the range of skills and competencies we have been talking about.

Can all these things really impact directly on learning in the classroom? Can they really affect what Year 3 will be doing next Thursday afternoon?

Yes they can. And the secret of how they do it is a tree.

SECTION II

How do we organise learning?

4 The curriculum tree

The Mystery of the Parish Register

A Year 6 History topic in an English primary school started with the teacher handing out photocopies of two pages of the local parish register. The first was from 1840, and the second from 1900. (Historians will have spotted that this was roughly the beginning and the end of Queen Victoria's reign.)

The teacher asked the children what they noticed. There is actually not much to notice in a parish register apart from 'John Smith of this parish married Wendy Jones of this parish', so the children very soon spotted that in 1840 everyone had married someone from the same parish. By 1900 well over half had married people from other parishes.

The teacher's response was to say, 'So, your job is to find out why' and then to add, 'How do you think you could do that?' The children talked in their groups and finally suggested: 'We'll go on the internet and find out' and 'We'll ask the vicar because he's in charge of the parish register'.

The third group said, 'We've been thinking about this and wondered if the change happened gradually or all at once in one year'. This is clearly a good question, so the teacher gave them the entire parish register.

The group with the parish register stuck pins in a map to show where a spouse had come from. This showed that until 1875 everyone had married someone from the same village. After 1875 the pins moved out to a circle of surrounding villages. They stayed there until 1880 when pins started appearing in a town about 20 miles away.

By the next day, the children had emailed the vicar, spoken to parents and others at home and pieced together the information from the internet. From this they came up with an explanation.

Have you spotted it? Yes, 1875 was about the time when bicycles had been invented, became more freely available and young men bought them, cycled to the next village, met girls and married them. It was 1880 when the railway was built to the town.

The teacher challenged the children to prove that these explanations were valid, and they came up with their own questions. Could Victorian bikes go so far? How long would it have taken? What leisure time did Victorians have for such pursuits? Could they all afford bikes?

They rode their own bikes to the villages on the map and timed the journeys. They found out about Victorian working hours and how fast bikes would have gone. They though about the conditions of the roads at that time and found the cost of bicycles – very expensive in relation to wages. This caused a second avenue of inquiry: can we find out how much different families earned? The answer lay in the census data and clinched the explanation. In almost every case, it was the richer families who married out of the parish. The railway explanation clinched itself: the dates corresponded, the railway went to only one nearby town, and villagers found their spouses in no other.

Part-way through the third day, the Victorian topic was completed.

The question from the first chapter was 'How do the wider aims, values, skills and competencies impact on the subjects?' How do we design a curriculum that enables children to acquire the skills, competencies, attitudes and values that they might need to face the 21st century, and also be inducted into the major subject areas that they also need in order to face that century. Are the two compatible? Do we have to make a choice, or compromise on one to achieve the other? And can we, at the same time, make learning exciting and engaging and challenging?

One way of approaching this issue is to think of the curriculum as being a tree (see Figure 4.1). In this tree we have 'branches of learning': Science, the Arts, Humanities and so on. These branches themselves branch out into smaller ones. Science branches into physics, chemistry and biology. Humanities branches into history, geography and citizenship and so on. This is just a way of thinking about the curriculum and seeing the connections.

At the end of the smaller branches (or twigs!) we find the leaves. The leaves are the individual bits of learning that are required by the National Curriculum or by the syllabus or course. So, if we go up the Humanities branch, and fork off along history, we shall find the Romans, Victorians and Incas and so on. If we go up the Science branch and then along physics, we get to 'electricity and magnetism' and 'forces'.

Most of our curriculum planning consists of arranging these leaves. Most of the thought that goes into reviewing a national curriculum is about what

Figure 4.1 The branches of learning

Figure 4.2 The whole curriculum

leaves we should have and what should be on them. In some cases, people look at the branches themselves and wonder if we need them all – or whether we need extra ones. Look at the lowest branch on the right that seems to have been chopped off. What do you think that would have been? Philosophy? Craft? Sociology?

Yet for all the time we spend thinking about the leaves, the model is incomplete. There's a bit under the ground. A bit we never see and so seldom think about. The bit that holds up all the rest and keeps it alive. The curriculum lacks roots.

Surely, the roots are where children learn to be critical thinkers and problem solvers, where they learn to work together in teams, develop their creativity and their social skills, learn to investigate, to evaluate, to develop new ideas, to be enterprising and to communicate in wide range of ways with a wide range of people. They also develop personally as confident individuals, willing to take risks, trying different methods and approaches, learning to deal with setbacks and difficulties. The roots are where children develop those additional Key Skills and 3C Competencies that we discussed in Chapter 2 (see Figure 4.2).

Looking at the curriculum in the context of this model, we begin to see how subjects and wider competencies, attitudes and dispositions can fit together. We also see that it is unnecessary to debate whether the curriculum should only be about subjects, or whether subjects are more important than skills. The tree needs both. The roots cannot develop without the photosynthesis in the leaves, and the leaves cannot grow without the moisture from the roots. They need each other.

Each of the skills, competencies, attitudes and dispositions at the root of learning needs the context of leaf to develop. Children cannot learn to solve problems unless they have some problems to solve – and those problems occur within the contexts of history, geography, science or technology or any other of the leaves. Children cannot learn to investigate unless they have something to investigate, and, again, the opportunities for investigation occur within the leaves. Children cannot learn to work together in teams unless the team has some enterprise in which to engage. None of the skills can be learned in a vacuum, and the subject disciplines, the established areas of human endeavour, mean that no such vacuum needs to exist.

This is not to say that the subject disciplines exist only to provide a context for the development of skills and competencies. They are important in their own right as knowledge frameworks and as ways of understanding the world. They are an essential part of being prepared for the 21st century. What the tree analogy makes clear is the symbiotic relationship between subject disciplines and skills. Children need the context of the subjects in order to develop the skills, and yet it is the skills that enable children to access the subjects. The two need each other and are inextricably intertwined.

The root of the problem

Interestingly, to pursue the analogy, an individual leaf is not always critical to the tree's health. A leaf could fall off, and the tree can grow a new one. In fact, all the leaves could fall off and if the tree has good roots it can grow a whole new set of leaves. This process could be repeated year after year – and wouldn't this be called 'Life-long Learning'? So isn't it the roots that promote life-long learning? The roots are the skills and competencies that enable them to continue learning, but also the attitudes and values that make them want to do so.

We can send a young person out into the world at 16 with a wonderful set of leaves, but if the roots are poorly developed, or if they have become 'pot-bound' because the curriculum has not allowed them to develop, then the young person has no grounding. At the first buffet of 21st century wind, that tree will blow over and the young person will become NEET (not in education, employment or training). What will sustain them through life are good roots.

Yet not only do we spend most of our time thinking about the leaves, and re-arranging the leaves and arguing about whether one leaf is more important than another, we also test children in terms of the leaves, and when the inspectors call, they also spend their time looking at the leaves. But when we asked people what they thought young people needed to equip them for the 21st century, they answered in terms of roots.

Harvard University once ran an experiment over several years in which they invited a representative sample of graduates to re-take their final examination a year later. Over 75 per cent failed. So we might conclude that there is little point in going to Harvard because a year later you will have forgotten everything you learned. But, of course, after three years at Harvard you are a different person: in terms of self-confidence, critical thinking, analysis, research, debate, discussion, explaining things, solving problems. In fact, all the roots. Yet it is not the roots that are tested. Of course, the graduates are much better versed in their own subjects as well – but not always enough to re-pass their finals!

There was an old saying that 'Education is what remains after you've forgotten all they taught you.' What remain, of course, are the roots.

And some fell on stony ground

At this point, some people will be saying, 'I accept the analysis – but it's not fair. In my school we are trying to lay down roots in particularly stony ground. Up the road, in the leafy suburb, it's really easy for the children to grow roots; in fact, they come to school at four with some roots already fairly well developed.' And this is true; which gives more weight to the model. Some children do come to school already able to co-operate and communicate, able to think critically to some extent and able to find out about things. They are curious and confident and want to find things out. So no wonder they find it easy to learn. Yet when children do not find it easy to learn, we do not always look to the roots as the reason; we more frequently concentrate on the leaves.

But it could well be that the very reason these young people are finding it hard to learn is that their 'roots' are not yet well established. Because they are not yet very good at co-operating, communicating, investigating, thinking critically or solving problems, and because they lack confidence to work independently, they find learning difficult. The leaves are failing to flourish because the roots are not well formed.

Once we start to look at the curriculum in this way, other things begin to fall into place. Not least the issue of curriculum design.

Looking at the trunk – the quality of children's learning experiences

What joins a tree's leaves to its roots is the trunk. In educational terms, the trunk is the quality of children's learning experiences. Some learning experiences are 'sterile' in that children gain a lot of knowledge about a 'leaf', but the experience does nothing to help them develop stronger roots. Other experiences are 'rich' in that they enable children to develop their understanding within a subject discipline, and also enable them to deepen and extend their roots as well.

In the example at the beginning of this chapter, children in Year 6 were learning about the Victorians, thus fulfilling a requirement of the English National Curriculum. In some schools this might have been a matter of amassing information about the Victorians – focusing on the 'leaf'. But here, the learning experience described goes beyond that. The children are learning about the Victorians, but at the same time they are developing their skills of solving problems, thinking critically (is the railway line really the reason for changing patterns of marriage?), investigating and working together in teams. Working in this way also helped them develop self-confidence and an ability to work independently.

But did this skill development detract from their learning of history? If we examine their learning of history in terms of the national requirements, we see that it was quite considerable. In terms of historical information, they found out about technological developments, work patterns, distributions of income and changing social patterns. In terms of historical skills, they used primary sources, analysed evidence and drew conclusions. They also did well in terms of the English National Curriculum Levels of Attainment. In this system, Level 3 requires children to know about 'the characteristic features' of the periods they study. Level 4 requires them to 'identify changes within and across the periods', and Level 5 expects them to 'give historical explanations' for those changes. They have grasped a key concept of history: developing technology impacts on social life.

The very design of this learning experience ensured that the children were working in the area of Level 4 because they were given parish register examples of a change. Their investigations revealed the historical explanations for these changes, which is Level 5 and so above the usual expectation for Year 6. The levels illustrated here are those of the English National Curriculum, but within any national system this represents progress in terms of historical understanding. The process can be adapted to any system.

The learning experience is rich because the roots of investigation, critical thinking and problem solving nourish the learning about Victorians. At the same time, the study of this aspect of Victorian life provides the context in which the 'roots' can develop. The 'trunk' of a rich learning experience brings the two together.

Is this the curriculum or teaching?

Some people might well wish to suggest that the parish register example is a matter of a particular teaching and learning approach, not a different curriculum. They are, of course, right in that the impact hinges around the approach, but in the definition of the curriculum set out in the first chapter, we said it was 'all the learning experiences the children receive as they go through the school'. By this definition, if you change the learning experience, you change the curriculum.

This is more than just playing with words. The Year 6 children in question could have completed their history topic by reading a textbook and completing a worksheet. They would have been complying (to a certain extent) with the National Curriculum requirement to study the Victorians, but their learning experience would have been very different from the pupils solving the mystery of the parish register, but who were also complying with the National Curriculum by studying the Victorians. As a result of the different learning experiences, the two sets of children will have learned different things. Not least, in terms of learning generic skills. But even the history they would learn would be different, even if it all fell under the heading of 'Victorians'. And if what they learn is different, then the curriculum is different.

Thus, the curriculum and the nature of teaching and learning are inextricably linked. You cannot change the one without changing the other. So there is a law of reciprocity here. A set of experiences (curriculum) that involves children working in co-operation, solving problems and finding things out will require different teaching and learning approaches from a set of learning experiences (curriculum) that involves children remembering facts and writing individually. And vice versa; different teaching and learning approaches will inevitably change the nature of the learning experience and so will change the curriculum.

If we change the learning experience, we change the curriculum. So if we want to change the curriculum, we need to change the very nature of the children's learning experiences.

How does this work at the design stage?

You can see the impact of this in the classroom, but how does it impact at the point of curriculum design?

One way of thinking about this is to see the two parts of the curriculum we have been talking about – subject disciplines (leaves) and a range of personal development, key skills and '3C' competencies (roots) – as forming a matrix. We can start the matrix with the subjects (see Figure 4.3). (Before you ask what's happened to ICT and Design and Technology – the diagram looked too crowded with them all in. They should be there and they are all important!)

We can then add the generic or key skills we see as important, or relevant to the particular group of children for whom we are designing these experiences (see Figure 4.4). In the process of curriculum design, a school or a teacher would take those skills that the children in that particular class needed to develop.

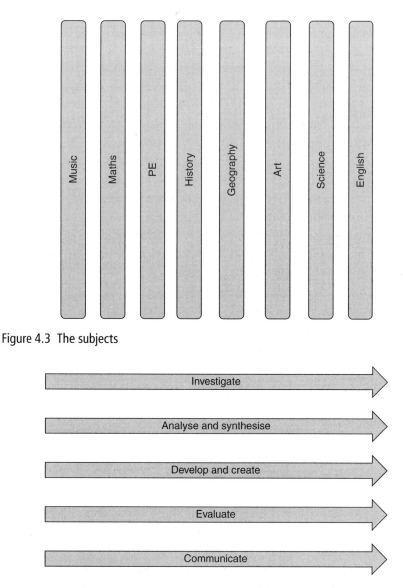

Figure 4.3 The subjects

Investigate

Analyse and synthesise

Develop and create

Evaluate

Communicate

Figure 4.4 The key skills

These are depicted as arrows because they run right through the curriculum and impact on all of the subject disciplines. Together they form the matrix (see Figure 4.5).

The key point of this model is that the key skills run right through all the subject disciplines. Creativity does not just happen in art, and communication does not just happen in English. The focus becomes the intersections, and the crucial question now becomes, 'How can Music help children

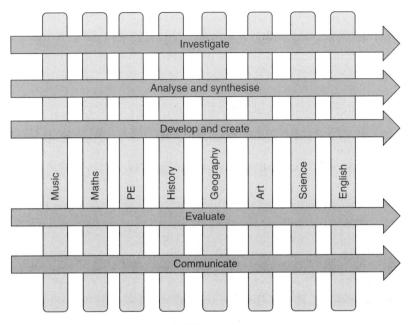

Figure 4.5 The matrix of subjects and skills

develop their investigation skills?', and 'How can Maths help them develop their creativity?' or 'How can Geography help with communication?' Of course, there is not a one-to-one match. Any subject discipline can help to develop any, or all, of the generic skills. It just depends how learning is put together. This is where flexibility and variation come in. All schools might be studying the Victorians, but the focus within that study will vary with the particular generic skills being developed. This will depend upon the children concerned and could vary from year to year. One class might be good at investigations but not at communication, and so the focus will shift.

This need not be a matter of 'diluting' the learning within the subject disciplines in order to 'shoehorn' in the generic skills. Approaching the subject disciplines through skills actually enhances children's learning of the subjects. It is not an 'either – or'.

The matrix in action

The key to using the matrix within curriculum design is for schools and teachers to use both elements when designing sets of learning experiences. In the parish register example, instead of setting out all the elements of the

Victorians (transport, houses, costume, the empire etc.) that could be covered within a given period of time and then arranging these elements into some sort of order, the teacher has used the skills as the key organiser for the experiences. If we want the children to develop their investigative skills, what aspects of the Victorians would be most useful to look at? Costume or housing would not be too useful here. But the connection between transport and social patterns is a rich source for investigations, and the parish register proved an ideal starting point.

The symbiotic relationship between 'roots and leaves' is also seen in action at this design stage. In order to provide intellectual challenge to these Year 6 children, we would expect them to go beyond the Level 3 requirement of knowing 'Characteristic features', and start to investigate the Level 4 element of 'Changes within and between periods'. The higher order demand is a much richer context for the development of investigational and problem-solving skills and so has the effect of increasing the level of demand. A focus on the 'content' of history (the leaves) instead of the generic skills is more likely to stick at the 'characteristic features' of Level 3. As a result of their investigations and their wrestling with the problem, the children almost inevitably attained Level 5 because the explanation was the whole purpose of the exercise.

Far from diluting, or detracting from, the subject learning, the skills organiser has actually enhanced subject learning. In fact, a series of experiences like this could well bring the children to Level 6: 'beginning to analyse the nature and extent of diversity, change and continuity within and across periods'.

Design triangles

The tree and the matrix are good models for seeing how all the elements of a curriculum fit together, but they are not very useful as tools of curriculum design. A more useful model in this context is the triangulation of the leaves and two aspects of the roots: Key Skills and Personal Development. The process can be illustrated as shown in Figure 4.6.

In the example at the beginning of this chapter, the children were learning history while developing their Key Skills of investigation, and also the Personal Development aspect of working together in teams. This could be illustrated as in Figure 4.7.

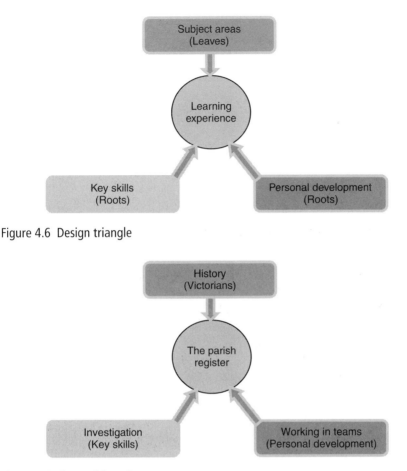

Figure 4.6 Design triangle

Figure 4.7 The parish register

The model has been presented retrospectively here, but could be used as a design tool, listing the skills that need to be developed, and the context in which they need to be developed. This triangulation will define the sort of learning experience needed: one that addresses all three.

If the children in your class are already good at investigation, but need to develop their information processing skills, and you still want to work within the same historical context, then the learning experience would change. What do you think it could be? What would promote all three? The process would look as in Figure 4.8.

You might, for example, show the children extracts from an early and late census, or the life expectancy figures across the century and ask them what they notice. It would take a bit of information processing to work out that

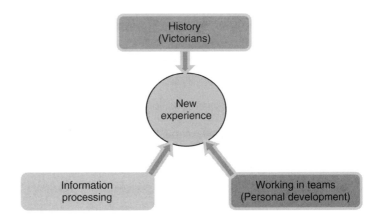

Figure 4.8 Information processing in the Victorian context

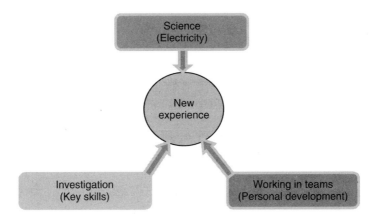

Figure 4.9 Investigating electricity

life expectancy increased towards the end of the century and that rates of infant mortality fell. The history remains the same: finding explanations for changes during the period. What has changed has been the bit of history that has been selected, and the skill that is being developed.

If we go back to the parish register example, we could have kept the two skills the same, but changed the subject, and again, another experience would be created.

This approach does not just work for history! How could we set these same skills in, say, science? What aspect of electricity would enable these skills to be developed? See Figure 4.9.

There are any number of experiences here, depending of the aspect of science being studied; for example, children could be asked to work in teams to find as many ways they can of varying the intensity of light coming from a bulb.

Making use of this approach

Curriculum planning meetings are often about making lists about all the things we want the children to learn. A curriculum design meeting would be about thinking up new experiences that would enable children to enhance their personal development and Key Skills in the context of subjects. In joining leaves to roots in this way, the trunk of learning always seems to become more challenging, more meaningful and more exciting. Children enjoy their learning, and learn more. And when they learn more, guess what? They do better in tests! You really can't go wrong!

The design process

We have been looking at how Key Skills can be built into design at a general level, but need to look more closely within skills and at how they fit with and support knowledge and understanding. We have not included the '3C Competencies' at this stage in order not to overcomplicate the picture. But they must also be part of the design, and in Chapter 9 we will look at how they form part of the design structure.

But before we get there, you may be thinking that all this is very well, but how can you design a curriculum in a different way when the national curriculum stops you. You may, of course, be a new English academy with no such constraints – but even so, it is worth looking at the next chapter and asking how much flexibility we have to arrange the curriculum in the way that best suits our pupils.

5 How can we design our own curriculum when we have to follow the national one?

The Skeleton

In one corner of the classroom is a skeleton grinning at the busy learners who have now grown too used to its presence to find it threatening or odd. Many of the skeleton's constituent parts have labels attached, and bones such as the 'tibia', 'fibula' and 'spine' can be identified. The label 'metatarsal' is attached to one of the bones in the foot, and a football boot sits next to it to give relevance to this piece of information.

In the other corner of the classroom is a plastic human torso with the front flapped open to reveal the internal organs. These are also labelled: heart, lungs, liver. Around the walls are charts of the human body showing the circulatory system with red arteries and blue veins.

So, what sort of classroom is this? Is it the first year of medical school? Are these learners aspiring doctors? But you already know the answer, because at some point in every year these will be found in a Key Stage 1 classroom near you. And you will know what's going on: it's the half term when the theme is 'Ourselves' or 'My Body'.

'It's all very well to talk about designing a rich curriculum with ambitious aims and ranges of 21st century skills and qualities – but here we are stuck with a national curriculum. So how are we supposed to do all these things when we we've got all these Programmes of Study to get through? In addition to that, I've got Ofsted coming next term, a SIP coming every term and SATs in May. There's just not time for these things, even though I can see that we should be doing them.'

In this chapter, we address this key issue, and explore what flexibility we have to design the curriculum we would want even within the apparent constraints we all face. There is a general feeling in most countries that the curriculum is something beyond the school's control, something that is imposed from above. If we are lucky, we can find a small amount of time to do the things we really want, but this time usually comes after SATs or on Friday afternoons and is not at the core of the school's work. This chapter will argue that we already have a great deal of flexibility to change the curriculum right now, and do not need to wait, or to become academies.

Where do the constraints come from?

This may seem too obvious to merit a section, but it is essential to think again about the impact of these upon the school. The economist John Maynard Keynes said that it is often difficult to grasp a new idea, but much more difficult to let go of an old one. So, before we embark on the task of designing our curriculum, it is important for us to examine some of our old ideas about the curriculum and the various forces that have combined to make it what it is. Only then can we see the flexibility we have to design a curriculum that includes our statutory requirements, but which does much more.

The English National Curriculum

The National Curriculum for Primary Schools in England is statutory, but the requirements of the statutes are much fewer, less precise and less restrictive than is generally supposed. This is true of the present Primary National Curriculum that will be in place until July 2013, and will be even truer when the revised and reduced curriculum is introduced in September of that year. We shall examine these later.

There are three distinct aspects to the perceived constraints of the National Curriculum:

- Content
- Time
- Rigidity

First, many schools feel that much of the content of the curriculum is not appropriate to the age or interests or needs of their pupils. The things we have to teach can seem too detailed or too remote to engage the children's interest or enthusiasm, or too removed from their needs and experience for them to understand. The result is a curriculum that often fails to connect with children's lives and their present level of understanding. To be successful, a curriculum must do more than merely fit with children's present lives, it must take them beyond those lives; it must widen their horizons, open their minds to new ideas and raise their aspirations. But to do so, it must start from where they are now. If it fails to connect with their lives, then it will leave them behind rather than take them to new places. The connection to their lives must be a hook that draws them into new worlds, new ideas and new understandings.

Second, there is a sense that the National Curriculum is too crowded, and there is just too much to get through. Schools tend to feel that the sheer amount that has to be covered does not allow any of it to be done properly. It seems that there is no time to follow the children's interests, or to enjoy reading stories or for practical or creative activities; time to explore and investigate, time to develop as individuals. Teachers feel under pressure to 'get through' or 'cover' or 'deliver' the Programmes of Study. The result is the sort of school curriculum we discussed in the previous chapter: children being rushed from one piece of learning to the next without time to think, let alone time to explore, investigate, understand and make connections.

Third, the National Curriculum is seen as imposing a rigid straightjacket that prevents learning being put together in ways that would appeal or make sense to children. It is set out in terms of ten subjects and so many schools feel obliged to teach it through those subjects and it can therefore seem too diverse to make sense as a coherent whole. The apparently rigid structure of subjects, attainment targets and key stages takes away the creativity, and even the professionalism, of teachers as curriculum designers. The result is a curricular uniformity that cannot take account of individual needs or local circumstances.

Does this sound familiar? But is it really the case?

In school after school, across the country, the curriculum is being put together in innovative, creative and exciting ways; ways that make learning exciting and relevant; ways that make time available for children to investigate and explore, to try out their own ideas and follow their own interests. How do these schools do it? How do they get round the statutory requirements of the National Curriculum?

Do we do far more than we need?

Let us look at the classroom with the skeleton and torso for an example. Is it really appropriate to expect 5- and 6-year-olds to know about the internal organs of the body and the bones of the skeleton? Doesn't this sound more like the first year of medical school? What is all the required learning that will take these young children so long to acquire? What is the actual statutory requirement that takes this half-a-term's work to cover?

We need to look at what is actually written in the Programmes of Study. In fact, there is only one sentence that refers to this piece of learning, and it is very short:

> Children should be taught the main external parts of the body of humans and animals.

That's all it says in the National Curriculum: 'the main **external** parts'. So we might ask why is there a skeleton and torso in every classroom during this topic when the requirement is to teach the **external** parts? Yet if you are familiar with Key Stage 1, you know that they are always there.

We might also ask which of external parts of the body are the **main** ones, and how many 'main parts' do children have to learn about? The Programmes of Study leave this open, but there is clarification in the Level Descriptions. There at Level 1 they state:

> Children should know the main external parts of the body of humans and animals (*for example,* head *and* arm).

So when we look at what the Programmes of Study actually say, we realise that the demand is in fact very reasonable both in terms of content and time. You might even think that it is not demanding enough. There cannot be many 5- or 6-year-olds who cannot already distinguish between their head and their arms.

If we read on through the Programmes of Study, we find that this is by no means an isolated example. In case after case, what has become standard practice in our primary schools far exceeds the expectations of the National Curriculum itself.

The huge demand perceived by schools in terms of content and time does not come from the National Curriculum itself. So where does it come from? What are the actual statutory obligations on schools with respect to the curriculum?

The statutory obligations

The statutory requirement on schools is to '*teach the Programmes of Study during the key stage*'. It is left up to the schools to decide how to teach the programmes of study, and how long to spend doing so. Let us look at the implications of this simple requirement.

Requirements of content

Schools are required to teach the Programmes of Study, but the previous section makes the case that these programmes are actually much less specific and demanding that most of us suppose. Where schools have gone back to the programmes and read them again, they always find that there is far less to cover than they thought, and also find that the demand is much more reasonable in terms of children's age and capabilities than they supposed.

It is important to note that the statutory requirements are *inclusive* but not *exclusive*. They say that the Programmes of Study must be taught, but they do not say that schools cannot teach other things as well. The programmes are a minimum entitlement for children, not a limit on what schools might teach.

This means that schools could teach Year 1 pupils about all the bones of the skeleton, or the circulatory system of the human body if they wanted to.

But it also means that they do not have to, and it certainly means that they do not have to spend half a term doing so if they do not want to do so.

Requirements of time

There have been various recommendations over the years from the government or public bodies about the amount time schools should spend on the National Curriculum, but none of these has been statutory. The Dearing Review of 1989 recommended an overall length of a week for primary schools (21 Hours for Key Stage 1 and 22.5 for Key Stage 2), and recommended that 80 per cent of that time should be spent on the National Curriculum. Within that 80 per cent, the Review recommended percentages of time for each subject. These recommendations were never statutory, but have seeped into to the consciousness of teachers and the practice of schools.

There is nothing in the statutory requirements, or even any recommendation, about how long schools should spend on different aspects of the programmes of study **within** a subject. In fact, the government publication 'Excellence and Enjoyment' (2003) reminded us that '*it is up to schools which aspects of the curriculum they do in depth. Some aspects might be covered in an afternoon.*' This publication has been in every primary school in England for over five years, but few schools have acted upon this part of its recommendations. It means that a school might spend only an afternoon on any of the aspects that usually take half a term. It certainly means that a school might spend only an afternoon ensuring that children knew about the main external parts of the body. (In fact, it is hard to see how this could take even an afternoon!)

Technically, there is no requirement to cover **any** aspect of the Programmes of Study in depth. They might all be covered in an afternoon each.

Requirements of structure

The statutory requirements leave it to schools to decide how to put the Programmes of Study together; whether to teach each aspect separately or to combine them, or whether to teach each aspect within subjects or to combine subjects. There is no regulation that requires schools to teach each of the ten subjects every week, or even every term or every year. The requirement is to teach the Programmes of Study during the key stage. This means, at a technical extreme, that all the programmes for maths could be taught at the beginning of Year 3 and not taught again until Year 7. Of course, no school would do this, and so no such regulation is needed. Teachers are professionals and know that mathematical understanding and skills need to be built up over time. But it does illustrate the extent of the flexibility that is available.

So the statutory requirements give schools much more flexibility than is usually supposed.

Within the Department for Education, there was an 'Innovations Unit', to which schools could apply for permission not to follow the National Curriculum, or to omit parts of it. The application usually meant setting out what the school would do instead that would be even more valuable. The interesting thing is that the Unit gave the same answer to 90 per cent of all applicants: 'You did not need to come to us for special permission; you have the flexibility and authority as a school to do that anyway.'

So 90 per cent of the schools that got round to applying to the Innovations Unit thought that the National Curriculum was more restrictive than it really was. And these are the schools that had presumably given a great deal of thought to the curriculum and were at the cutting edge of innovation. Yet even they did not realise how much flexibility and control they actually had.

So why do more schools not take advantage of the flexibilities offered by the present National Curriculum? Why do they go into more detail than they need, or introduce more content than they need? Why do they spend more time than they need? Why do they keep to a structure that is not actually required?

So why do we do so much more than we need?

The key to understanding why so many schools feel that there is too much in the National Curriculum, but then do more than they need, is to look at the various influences that have shaped the way in which schools understand and interpret the National Curriculum. In many cases, schools have not looked at the Programmes of Study for many years. They therefore interpret them in terms of the many support materials, strategies and planning guides that have been issued and the courses they have attended. A view of the National Curriculum has grown up within the profession that is almost mythic. There is a strong belief about what is required and the amount of time to be taken and the structures to be used that bears little relation to the statutory requirements. And to unravel these and to get back to what will be best for children, we need to examine those various influences that have brought this about.

QCA schemes of work

It seems really odd that in so many schools Key Stage 1 classes spend a long time teaching young children about skeletons and internal organs when they do not want to, and then complain that they struggle to fit everything in. It seems really odd until you look at the QCA Schemes of Work. There you find the reason. The QCA Unit suggests the study of the skeleton, even though it is not a requirement of the relevant Programme of Study or the associated Level Description. The unit also recommends 12 hours of study, so seems to suggest that there must be much more to teaching children about the main parts of the body that one might reasonably suppose by reading the Programmes of Study themselves.

Many schools still see the QCA Schemes of work as the National Curriculum itself. Teachers consult the schemes of work frequently and work from them in their planning and so are very familiar with them. In many cases, it is a long time since teachers looked at the National Curriculum itself. So they come to think that everything in a QCA Scheme of Work is a statutory requirement, when in fact the schemes are not statutory at all. So when schools say that there is far too much to do in the National Curriculum, they really mean that there is far too much in the QCA Schemes of Work.

'Upping the ante'

Not only do most of the Schemes of Work go way beyond the requirements of the Programmes of Study in terms of extent of content, level of demand and time to be taken, they also embody a planning structure that has become prevalent in primary schools:

- Learning objectives
- Teaching activities
- Learning outcomes

All the Units have a subject focus, and although they point to links to other subjects, these are seldom integral to the learning experience. At no point do the schemes illustrate how generic skills can be developed in the context of the subject.

In going beyond the requirements of the Programmes of Study in this way, the QCA Schemes of Work have set the standard for curriculum planning, and in doing so have considerably 'raised the ante' in terms of content and time. It has become almost the norm to think of the different aspects of the Programmes of Study in terms of how they might be translated into 'teaching activities' that are akin to the Schemes of Work. This has implied a structure to the curriculum that is neither an explicit nor implicit part of the National Curriculum.

The QCA Schemes of Work were produced for guidance and exemplification. They never were statutory, and it was never expected that any school would do them all. Yet they have played a significant part in shaping the way schools view the National Curriculum and interpret its demands.

Even though the QCA itself is abolished, and its website shut down, the interpretation the Schemes of Work embodies will remain powerful within the profession until we go back to the Programmes of Study and look again at what they actually say. We then need to think what this really means in terms of children's learning, rather than how can we use this requirement as a starting point to plan learning experiences that are in the style of a QCA Scheme of Work.

This will still pertain when the new National Curriculum is published. There will be an inevitable tendency to interpret it in terms of the present curriculum and the old Schemes of Work – Keynes has warned us of this! What we need to do is to look at it afresh and interpret the requirements in terms of the pupils in front of us, and what they know, can do and understand, and how this new learning will fit within their lives.

The QCA Schemes of Work have been very influential in shaping how we view the National Curriculum. But they have not been the only influence.

Early Ofsted inspections

Ofsted inspections of primary schools started in 1992 and some of the early inspections were very demanding in terms of the paperwork they required from schools. With four days in a school and large teams, inspectors had plenty of time in the early days to look in detail at plans and 'evidence' of the curriculum that children were following. Ofsted issued guidance to its inspectors about the features of a 'good' and 'excellent' curriculum. Like the QCA Schemes of Work, these guidelines went far beyond the statutory requirements of the National Curriculum. Schools were required to fill in forms about how many minutes a week they spent teaching each subject, even though there was no requirement to teach every subject every week, or even teach in subjects at all. The form itself became influential in shaping thinking along these lines. In many cases, inspectors demanded a level of detail in planning and 'coverage' that was also beyond any statutory requirement. The overall impact was to paint a portrait of a national curriculum that was demanding in content, in time and in structure. This portrait has been significant in shaping thinking about the curriculum.

Ofsted requirements have changed significantly since those early days, and now the criteria for an 'outstanding curriculum' has moved thinking very far forward. However, there is a 'perceptual inertia' within schools which means that, even though the criteria have changed, schools still tend to think that Ofsted are looking for detail and compliance rather than the actual criteria which are:

> The school's curriculum provides memorable experiences and rich opportunities for high-quality learning and wider personal development and wellbeing. The school may be at the forefront of successful, innovative curriculum innovation . . .

Of course, Ofsted has no authority to set requirements for schools at all. It can only set requirements for its own inspectors to follow when they write their reports. However, these reports are influential on schools, so there is a tendency for schools to take notice of what Ofsted says. But, interestingly, just like the National Curriculum itself, schools seem more influenced by what they **think** Ofsted will say than they are by the criteria themselves. How many schools have read the criteria for an outstanding curriculum and said to themselves, 'We really must show the inspection team that we are at the forefront of innovation?'

It is odd how the influences tend to take so many schools away from what they think the curriculum should be and make the curriculum more extensive in terms of content and time, and more rigid in terms of structure. Perhaps the greatest influence in this direction has been the National Strategies.

The National Literacy and Numeracy Strategies

These were introduced to give schools some strategies to implement the requirements of the National Curriculum and, by so doing, raise standards in literacy and numeracy. They were never statutory, but their influence on primary schools has been deep and extensive. Although they have now been abandoned, their influence lingers on.

The National Curriculum specifies English and Mathematics rather than literacy and numeracy, so the very names heralded a shift in emphasis. The original Literacy Strategy omitted the Speaking and Listening attainment target of English altogether. Yet many people see this as a fundamental aspect of English in a primary school. The initial Numeracy Strategy focused on the Number and Algebra attainment targets of Mathematics. So from the start there was immediately an implication that not only are English and Maths more important than other subjects, but that some aspects of these subjects were more important than others.

The impact on schools' interpretation of the content and time requirement was significant. The Strategies 'pulled out' aspects of their chosen attainment targets into lessons with very specific content and which spanned all six years of Key Stages 1 and 2 and provided lessons for every day of the week for the whole year. To do so they inevitably extended many simple and straightforward requirements of the Programmes of Study into unnecessarily long, complex and detailed series of lessons which stray far from the needs of either young children or the National Curriculum. For example, a requirement in the Key Stage 2 Writing Programme of Study states that:

> *Children should be taught to write for different purposes and audiences.*

To help schools teach this element, the National Literacy Strategy introduced the notion that there are 6 'Genres' in which children are supposed to be able to write (Stories, Accounts, Poems, Descriptions, Diaries, Articles). But this is far beyond the National Curriculum requirement. Nowhere does it say that children should be able to write in different 'genres'. This is a very technical requirement that is not present in the primary school curriculum of any other country in the world. It is not even in the Programmes of Study for Key Stages 3 or 4. Yet across the country we now have young children trying to write in different genres, when what they should be doing is thinking about who they are writing for, and whether different purposes need different forms to be effective.

The worry is that even though the National Strategies have now been abandoned, there will still be children being taught to write in six genres. And there will be newspapers saying that children are leaving school unable to write because they can only manage four genres instead of six.

The implications for rigidity of structure were twofold. Both strategies specified that their subject should be taught daily, and at first suggested that they should be taught as separate subjects. And both strategies were based on the structure of a three-part lesson.

Later 'refreshings' of the strategies moved away from these structures, and suggested that literacy and numeracy were best taught in the context of other subjects, but, interestingly, these later revisions seemed to have far less impact on primary school practice than the initial, more rigid strategies. In many schools, there are still separate daily literacy and numeracy sessions based on a three-part lesson, and this lesson structure is even applied to other subjects as well.

The impact has been pervasive as well as extensive, and seems to be remaining even though the strategies have been abandoned. Of course, they were never statutory in the first place, but they have been more influential than some aspects of the National Curriculum that have always been statutory.

Putting pressure on ourselves

As if there was not enough external pressure on schools to shape the curriculum in ways we may not want, we tend to put extra pressure on ourselves as schools and as teachers.

Head teachers often require teachers to submit termly or half-termly curriculum plans that show in considerable detail what is going to be taught in each subject. Heads do have an obligation to ensure that the Programmes of Study are being taught during the key stage, but the submission of such plans is neither the only nor the best method of achieving this. We shall look at alternative ways in Chapter 8.

When they review the plans that their teachers submit, very few heads send them back saying 'This is far too much', or asking 'Why are you planning all this?' In fact, very few heads comment at all on the quality of the curriculum embodied in the plans, because the focus tends to be on compliance. Yet it is vitally important for heads to be active in shaping the curriculum as it develops.

Heads are generally assisted in their role by a range of subject leaders, all of whom make demands in terms of planning, and who are often focused on ensuring that their subject is properly represented in the whole curriculum. They often produce the plans that teachers follow, or on which they base their own lessons.

At the bottom of the pile is the class teacher following advice and guidance and producing ever more complex and detailed plans. At this level, we feel the double pressure of producing all the planning that seems to be required by those above us, and then trying to implement these plans in the classroom. As teachers, we often feel that there is far too much to do in the curriculum, but the sheer amount often comes from our own plans, not from the National Curriculum. As we have often produced these plans for others, rather than for ourselves, it is not always easy to make them what we want. But until we do so, we shall never have the curriculum we want, or that the children need.

It really is time to call a halt to this process if we are to design a curriculum that works for our pupils in our situations, and the rest of this book will be about how to do just that. But before we move on, we must look at one final 'old idea' that we really need to let go of: the half-term time slot.

The half-term time slot

The skeleton and torso were part of a half-term topic or theme. It would be surprising to a visitor from elsewhere to find that all aspects of the English Primary National Curriculum seem to take exactly half a term. Have you noticed it? When we do 'The Victorians', it takes exactly half a term. Then 'Rivers' take half a term as well. As do 'Forces' or 'Habitats'. Some schools have wider themes such as 'Where do we come from?' or 'Our Planet, Earth'; but whatever the theme, it always seems to take exactly half a term.

The really odd thing is – it doesn't seem to matter how long the half a term is. One year, Easter is late and so we spend seven weeks on 'The Victorians' with Year 5. The next year, Easter is early, the same half-term is only four weeks long – but the Victorians still fit in! How does that happen? Where do the extra three weeks go? Why does everything always seem to take half a term? Could we always do the Victorians in four weeks and use the other three for something else? Perhaps we could always do the Victorians in even less than four weeks.

Planning in half-term chunks has two key disadvantages. First, it makes some pieces of learning far longer (or shorter) than is necessary for children to grasp the key points of what is being taught. Second, having a fixed slot, however long it is, means that the planning process tends to be one of filling the slot, rather than thinking about what experiences children will need in order to grasp the intended learning, and then thinking how long that will take. The slot tends to get filled with activities rather than focus on the key experiences that children need. We know when a topic or theme is over because we have a holiday, and when we come back we start something new.

As a result of the National Strategies and other initiatives, we are all very sure to have clear learning objectives for each lesson. But we seldom have such clear objectives for longer pieces of work. That's why we need a holiday to tell us that the topic is finished. If we had clearer longer-term learning objectives, the topic would be finished when the objectives were met. We shall be looking at this further in Chapter 13.

The way forward

During the writing of this book, a wide range of initiatives is being reviewed by the Government with a promise to sweep them all away, and to reduce the overall statutory requirement on schools. But none of the initiatives were statutory in the first place, so the situation will not materially have been changed. It is true, of course, that the mere act of removing these initiatives from the various websites will greatly reduce the pressure on schools to do something about them, and if the Secretary of State writes to schools to say they no longer exist that will also be significant.

But the removing of the initiatives will not clear the way for us to design the curriculum that we want if we are still trapped in the thinking that those initiatives embodied. We are standing at the beginning of a wonderful opportunity to rethink the curriculum and to make it one of which we can all be proud. To make the most of that opportunity we must not only grasp the new ideas, but also let go of the old ones.

Whatever the new National Curriculum says, it will be schools that interpret it into learning experiences for children. To do this, it is necessary to look at the National Curriculum itself, and to interpret that in the light of the statutory requirements. It is necessary to get away from what we *think* it says or what we assume we are supposed to do. By doing this, we shall find that there is plenty of flexibility to put the curriculum together in ways that are exciting and engaging for children; that connect with their lives and yet take them to the places they have never been. These are the rich experiences that link leaves to roots and provide for the development of the whole child. This is the way in which we enable children to explore their world and find their place within it.

These cultivate the deep roots of learning.

6

The deep roots of learning

The Nail Bar

Two prospective business people sit nervously as their business plan is scrutinised by a bank manager. He asks them what the impact would be on their profit margin if the cost of their raw material increased by 10 per cent. They do the calculation and can give the figure. 'At what point would you need to raise your prices before you made a loss?' They are ready for this and have worked on a 20 per cent margin. The raw material is expensive, but they will use little of it relative to labour and expertise. Once they have gained the bank manager's approval, they are ready to set up their new enterprise.

The prospective business people are two 10-year-old girls who are setting up a 'nail bar' as part of the school's fund-raising fair. All children have been asked to submit ideas, but also to complete business plans with market and cost analyses, input implications and profit forecasts. Local banks have agreed to participate by subjecting the plans to scrutiny. They have been primed to ask certain questions of different pupils depending on the stage of learning. The questions focus on aspects of mathematics that the children are learning at that time. In the case of the nail bar, it was percentages. The normal scrutiny of the plan's feasibility reveals that the girls have visited nail bars to see one in action, have received some training from an experienced adult, have taken account of health and safety aspects and have given thought to customer care and relationships.

> The nail bar was a success at the fair, but afterwards the girls were approached by people wanting their nails done at home. The school enterprise became a real enterprise. The really heartening aspect of the story is that both girls were from families where no one had been employed for two generations, yet as 10-year-olds they were already running a business.

If we have much more flexibility than most of us thought, and if we recognise in the tree analogy that there are roots to learning as well as leaves of content to cover, then we not only have time to consider those roots, we also have a model by which we can build them into curriculum design. This we can do even if the National Curriculum were to change in a national review, and even if the new National Curriculum seems to contain nothing but leaves. It will still be our responsibility as schools to ensure that our pupils receive a broad, balanced and rounded education that prepares them fully for the future. This is why the way we design the curriculum is so important.

There are two important points in the consideration of roots:

- They are a significant part of learning and so should be a significant part of design.
- Designing the curriculum this way deepens learning itself.

There is a notion of 'deep learning' that takes learning beyond superficial memorisation to more complex understanding. This has been dealt with by writers from Piaget (1950) and Bruner (1966) to Hargreaves (2006), all of whom stress the need to take learning beyond the disconnected, superficial and transient, and let it become meaningful, deep and lasting.

Bloom's taxonomy

Many countries still use Bloom's 1956 *Taxonomy of Learning Objectives* in their approach to curriculum design. Bloom suggested that within the cognitive domain, there is a hierarchy of processes. Bloom saw three sorts of 'knowledge', and these rise through this hierarchy. The first is 'knowing that' (the recall of information). The second is 'knowing how to', which suggests skills. The third is 'knowing about', which is grasping the principles and generalisations. (This causes a directional conflict of the metaphors! We talk of 'deep learning', while Bloom talks of a rising scale of 'higher order' abilities. 'Higher' or 'deeper'? These are just metaphors to refer to learning that goes beyond the superficial. Some people use the term 'profound learning'.)

Whether we use a metaphor of 'higher' or 'deeper' or call it 'profound learning', the important thing is the order of the hierarchy, which Bloom suggests is (in ascending order):

- Recall
- Comprehension
- Application
- Analysis
- Synthesis
- Evaluation

Bloom suggests that 'recall' is the most superficial level and that deeper learning involves doing something with that recall, and taking children through the stages. Bloom uses the word 'knowledge' in a specialised way to include recall of information, knowledge of ways of dealing with information, and knowledge of principles and generalisations. This is why we use the terms 'recall' or 'remembering' for the superficial stage.

Several people have sought to 'update' this taxonomy, and one update that is widely used is by one of Bloom's pupils, Lorin Anderson in 2001. Anderson basically turned the nouns to verbs, merged analysis and synthesis and added creativity. The hierarchy then becomes:

> Remembering, comprehending, applying, analysing, evaluating and creating

In terms of the 'tree' model, the first two (remembering and comprehending) are the leaves, so it is the addition of the roots that 'deepens' the learning by moving it from the superficial to the higher order level (see Figure 6.1).

It is when children start to apply their recall and comprehension, when they begin to analyse the information they have acquired, to evaluate its worth and then to use the information creatively, that they have taken it to the deep (or high!) level of full conceptual development. The word we usually use for this deep conceptual level is 'understanding'.

The implication of this analysis for curriculum design is that children need to be engaged with their learning at the levels of the application of skills for the learning to be deep. Lessons where children sit passively absorbing

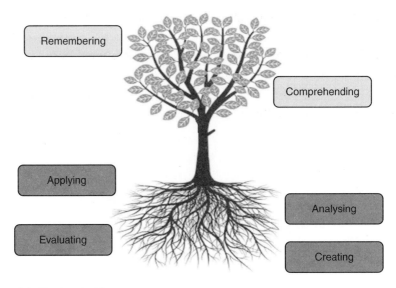

Figure 6.1 The tree in bloom

information will leave them at best at the level of comprehension. The deep learning that comes from the application of skills needs the active engagement of the learner. So we need to design experiences that give this opportunity.

Marton and Saljo

In 2008, Marton and Saljo of Gothenburg University considered 'Deep and Surface Approaches to Learning' and saw three levels, which they likened to coffee moving through the cafetiere to make the final brew. This is an interesting metaphor, because we often try to speed up the coffee process by trying to ram it down with the plunger – but when it is ready it sinks of its own accord. Then all you have to do is rest your finger on the plunger and it sinks gently. And you get much better coffee if you wait for it to have infused properly! This might conjure up an image of unfortunate children having learning rammed down their throats, when the teacher would be better advised to give them time to explore their learning and to let it sink in. The ramming down their throats will not make good learning anyway.

Marton and Saljo's three levels are as shown in Figure 6.2.

- Memorising facts
- Learning to pass exams
- Learning detached from the real world

- Questioning
- Changing ways of thinking
- Engaging with learning

- Searching for meaning
- Approaching learning from the real world
- An holistic approach to learning

Figure 6.2 Deep and surface approaches to learning

Making it work in school

The notion of 'deep learning' was also addressed in a series of papers for the Specialist Schools and Academies Trust (SSAT) by David Hargreaves in 2006. Hargreaves argues that deep learning is brought about by the greater involvement of the learner in the process, so that they become active agents in their own learning rather than remain passive recipients of teaching. He sees this as the process of 'personalising' learning. In this analysis, to achieve deep learning, it is necessary to provide what Hargreaves calls:

- Deep experiences
- Deep support

This requires changes both in curriculum design and the in nature of teaching and learning to create the 'co-construction of learning'. This co-construction can be carried out between teacher and pupil, and between pupil and pupil. Hargreaves sees a cycle around student learning, as shown in Figure 6.3.

Hargreaves' paper was written for secondary schools, so the notion of 'maturity' would need to be interpreted in terms of primary children rather than secondary students, but the notion of progressive deepening through student engagement is still useful.

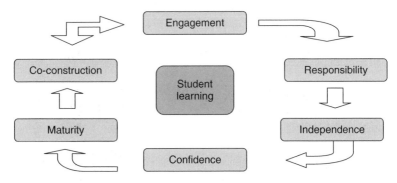

Figure 6.3 Hargreaves' cycle

Hargreaves' notion of 'co-construction' involves the active engagement of the learner. Learning moves from the passive to the active, and involves responsibility and independence as a route to maturity and co-construction.

Deep learning in action

The children setting up their nail bar are engaging in the co-construction of learning, and so, in Hargreaves' terms, deepening it. In terms of Bloom's amended taxonomy, they are also operating at the highest (deepest!) level of creativity, having applied their learning, analysed and evaluated all they have found out about running a nail bar, and have set that in the context of other learning at school.

In fact, all the examples we have looked at so far (and will see in future chapters) also go a long way down in terms of the roots, and so achieve deep learning.

The nature of knowledge

Seeing skills as the way in which knowledge and understanding are deepened makes the continuing debate about whether knowledge is more important than skills even more pointless. It has been noted that some of the debate comes from the contrast between the rather strict view that knowledge is the possession of information ('knowing that'), and the more common-sense view, that knowledge implies 'knowing all about' something. In Dicken's 'Hard Times', the teacher Gradgrind says that his pupil Sissy Jupe does not know what a horse is because she cannot recite the dictionary definition of one. Sissy, of course, knows all about horses as her family keeps them, and she looks after them.

This Dickensian divide is still driving educational debate in England. Presumably, no one would oppose the 'deep knowledge' that Sissy has of horses. And no one would advocate the superficial memorisation of Gradgrind's 'facts'. Yet there seems to be a feeling among some non-educationalists that there is insufficient 'knowledge' in the National Curriculum, or being taught in schools. This may be because there are few 'facts' listed in the national Programmes of Study. This is mainly because there are so many facts that a child learns by the age of 11 that it is impossible to list them all. If we were to attempt to list all the things that Sissy knew about horses, the list would be immense. It would certainly exceed the pupil Bitzer's definition that so pleased Gradgrind: '*Quadruped. Graminivorous. Forty teeth, namely twenty-four grinders, four eye-teeth, and twelve incisive. Sheds coat in the spring; in marshy countries, sheds hoofs, too. Hoofs hard, but requiring to be shod with iron. Age known by marks in mouth.*'

This is the reason that the national Programmes of Study so frequently use the phrase 'pupils should be taught about . . .', rather than 'Pupils should be taught that . . .'. Learning 'about' something implies not only a wider range of knowledge, but it also implies that the knowledge is sorted into some order. This moves the knowledge from Bloom's first to second stage of comprehension. It is impossible to prescribe every piece of information that a child should acquire. So specifying that children should 'learn about' certain things actually *increases* the amount of knowledge they will learn, as they will almost certainly learn more than could be prescribed. What is lost in this transaction, of course, is total control of the specific knowledge being acquired. It may well be this desire for control that is fuelling the debate about knowledge, whatever is being said about freedom and flexibility.

Sissy Jupe's knowledge about horses did not come from Mr Gradgrind's lessons. It came from her first-hand experiences in practical situations that were relevant to her life; experiences in which she was guided by more experienced people who were important to her, and to which she had emotional commitment. She was mixing skills with knowledge. She was applying her knowledge to looking after her horses and so deepened her learning.

The third form of knowledge is 'knowing how' to do something. This always suggests a skill rather than informational or conceptual knowledge, but it is part of common usage. There is even an element of uncertainty here: Is knowing how to do something the same as being able to do it? For example, you may know how to play darts: you stand on the line and throw the dart so that it sticks in the board. However, that does not mean that the dart will hit the board when you throw it, or stick in the board if it hits it. It certainly doesn't mean it will stick in the treble twenty. This meaning of 'knowing how' is not the same as 'being able to'.

There are many lessons where children are still being taught in way that will enable them to answer questions, or even to do well in tests, but not to apply the things they are learning. They can tell you how to play darts, but cannot throw a dart themselves. The children are stuck at the superficial level of Bloom's second stage.

It is only when knowledge is 'knowing about' and is acquired in the context of the application of skills that we will achieve deep learning. This needs a holistic approach.

A holistic approach

The analysis that sees skills as a way of deepening learning sees the skills as integral to the development of knowledge and understanding. There is often a question about whether skills should be taught separately, and then applied in context, or whether they should be learned in the context in which they will be applied. The answer to this, like the answer to many design questions, is: 'both', but depending on the context and learner.

The danger of teaching a skill in isolation from its context of use is three-fold. The first point is that the child may not see the point of the skill in isolation and so fail to comprehend what the skill is for. In an adult context, it is pointless trying to teach someone how to finesse in the card game bridge before the player can see why you would ever need to do so. After you have lost your Queen to your opponents' King a few times even though you held the Ace, you will fully understand what is going on and so be ready to learn the skill. The second point is that you will also be keen to learn the skill because you have gained some emotional commitment to learning. Finally, there is growing evidence that skills learned in context are much more likely to be able to be applied in context.

This is why we often give children the opportunity to explore new materials or talk about new situations before we start instruction. 'Have a go and see what you can do.' Or 'How do you think we could do this?' This gives the children some context in which they can understand the new learning; some pegs on which they can hang new ideas. Without this initial familiarity with a new context, new ideas and information are often meaningless. This is why children sometimes simply do not understand something, even though the explanation seems so clear. In technical terms, they do not have a mental 'schema' that allows them to accommodate the new information.

This is not to say that there will not be times when it will be necessary to teach a skill before experiencing the context of its application. Using a chainsaw is usually given as an example of learning where exploratory methods would be inappropriate. However, even here the new user will always have some idea about the context of cutting and using handtools. There will also be times when we need to stop and think about why things are not going right. This is the time when the need for the skill becomes apparent, when the children understand the context, and will have a commitment to learning it. At this point, the skill is taught separately, but only because the context has already been fully established, and will be there ready for the skill to be practised immediately before the learning is lost.

Have you ever stood in a group around a computer while someone demonstrates some new program or technique? By the time you get to use the new program yourself, you always seem to have forgotten what they said. You need to use the new techniques straight away in order for them to become embedded.

Being embedded means the learning was deep.

Within the subject areas, there is also deep subject learning that takes the curriculum beyond superficial content. This is the subject of the next chapter.

7 A canopy of leaves – the subject disciplines

Life's a Beach

A class of 10-year-olds spent the day at the beach. They explored the life in rock pools, and took photographs of the things they saw. They filmed the patterns the waves make on the sand and the way the cliffs are being eroded. They met fishermen, and made a video of their discussions with them about their life and work. They visited the old lighthouse and were taken up to the lamp room.

Back in school the next day, they discussed how to sort out this information to put it on the class website. They found out about the flora and fauna they had seen in the rock pools. They found more examples of erosion, and checked out about typical catches and marketing by fishermen. They found out more about lighthouses and navigational aids, and, in a concession to the past, they made a model of a lighthouse with a light that flashed in the same pattern as the one they had seen, and set it against a photo-shopped background.

What subject were they doing?

In Chapter 1, we spoke about children needing to set out on their journey through life, and also to take account of the accumulated knowledge and experience of all those people who have gone before. That accumulated knowledge and experience has been stored and catalogued over the centuries. The systems of categorisation and storage have varied with those centuries. Medieval universities in Europe studied medicine, law, theology and the liberal arts. The latter were seen as arithmetic, geometry, astronomy, music theory, grammar, logic and rhetoric.

Over the years, knowledge has grown and been constantly reclassified into different groups or subjects. These subjects, or 'subject areas', are more than stores of knowledge. They have created structures for understanding that knowledge, and have developed methodologies for accumulating new knowledge. These are systems of thought into which children have a right to be inducted. In medieval times, an educated elite kept the masses in ignorance. Education is about the right of every human being to have access. This is the role of the curriculum.

Back on the beach, the small human beings are busily accessing knowledge. What subject were they studying? We all know the answer to this question. The children were clearly engaged in many subjects at once, and we do not need to list them. The issue is whether subjects are helpful and essential disciplines, or whether they get in the way of the sort of organic and joined-up learning that happened on the beach. Is it better to mix subjects up like this or to study them separately?

There is a general perception that before the National Curriculum was introduced in 1989, English primary schools tended to arrange the entire curriculum in themes. The situation probably existed more in the perception than in the reality. When Neville Bennett carried out his research for *Teaching Styles and Pupil Progress* in 1976, he struggled to find a representative sample of 'progressive' schools pursuing a thematic approach. This was confirmed by a survey carried out by Her Majesty's Inspectors of Schools (HMI) (*Primary Schools in England* 1976) in the same year. They found that there was certainly some use of thematic approaches, but the great majority of schools taught most subjects discretely. Of course, some things such as swimming and much of PE are hard to do in any other way. But, despite the evidence to the contrary, the perception remained that children were taught everything though 'Topics'. There was a then a reaction to this 'Topic-based approach' which became to be seen as 'woolly' and lacking rigour.

There was also a concern that children were failing to master any of the 'subject disciplines', which were seen as underpinning human understanding and providing the rigour and coherence lacking in thematic approaches. The introduction of a National Curriculum sought to address these issues by setting out clearer expectations for subjects and within subjects, and many primary schools now group learning into subjects to an even greater extent than they did before.

Another key objective of the National Curriculum was to ensure a minimum entitlement for all children, and this is an important concern of curriculum design. Articulating a range of subjects is one way of ensuring breadth of study and ensuring that all children will have access to a rounded education.

But does this require the subjects to be taught separately? Or can children benefit from a life on the beach? Does it have to be an 'either – or'? Is there a right and wrong here? As with other educational issues raised so far, the real answer is that it needs to be both.

There is a need for children to be 'inducted' into the subject disciplines. These are the major systems of human thought, and the ways in which society has stored its wisdom. They are bodies of accumulated knowledge, and they are also structures for understanding that knowledge, and systems of finding new knowledge within those structures. More of this below.

But children also need to see the connection between one subject discipline and another. In order to understand the world fully and be able to operate effectively within it they need to see its interconnectedness and realise that not only does one thing impact upon another, but that looking at life through more than one lens enhances understanding.

Many countries take account of this double need in their National Curricula. Finland and New Zealand are among many countries to make specific reference to the need for integration, as seen in Figures 7.1 and 7.2.

English primary schools have the same freedom and flexibility. There is no statutory requirement to teach the curriculum as separate subjects. So we

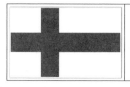

Instruction may be separated into subjects or integrated. The objective of integration is to guide pupils in examining phenomena from the perspective of different fields of knowledge, thereby elaborating themes and emphasising general educational goals.

Figure 7.1 Finland

While the learning areas are presented as distinct, this should not limit the ways in which schools structure the learning experiences offered to students. All learning should make use of the natural connections that exist between learning areas and that link learning areas to the values and key competencies.

Figure 7.2 New Zealand

need to decide whether to do so or not, or whether to teach parts of subjects separately and some in connection with others. And we need to establish the grounds for making these decisions. To do this we need to look at the subjects themselves.

Statutory integration

In some countries, cross-curricular themes are a required part of the national curriculum, so schools are required to spend at least some of their time teaching subjects through themes. It is interesting to note that some countries that do very well in international comparisons in terms of subjects also require cross-curricular themes. For example, Finland requires seven cross-curricular themes, as listed in Figure 7.3.

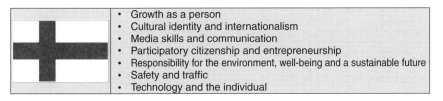

- Growth as a person
- Cultural identity and internationalism
- Media skills and communication
- Participatory citizenship and entrepreneurship
- Responsibility for the environment, well-being and a sustainable future
- Safety and traffic
- Technology and the individual

Figure 7.3 Finland's cross-curricular themes

Can we do this in England?

In Chapter 2, we looked at the list of subjects that has been the English National Curriculum since 1989 and noted that the list had changed little from 1905. This gives the list an air of permanency and authenticity. But when we look in detail, it is not as fixed and permanent as it seems. Not all countries have the same list. Some countries include other subjects; for example, Philosophy is compulsory in France, and most countries include a modern foreign language at primary level. Some countries omit some subjects on the English list, or arrange them in different ways; for example, many countries list 'Social Studies' rather than history and geography, and much of what is in geography in England is found in Science in other countries (rocks, erosion, climate etc.). Many countries start with broad areas of

Singapore	New Zealand
Mother tongue English Maths Civics and moral education Art and craft Music Health education Social studies Physical education Science (From Grade 4)	English Other language The arts Health and physical education Maths and statistics Science Social science Technology

Figure 7.4 Areas of learning

Table 7.1 Alexander and Rose: Areas of learning

Alexander	Rose
Arts and creativity	The Arts
Science and technology	Science and technology
Mathematics	Mathematics
Language, oracy and literacy	English, communication and languages
Place and time	Historical, geographical and social (includes citizenship)
Citizenship and ethics	
Physical and emotional health	Physical development, health and well-being
Faith and belief	

learning for younger children and move to more specialised subjects later; for example, we can see a comparison of the curricula of Singapore and New Zealand in Figure 7.4.

New Zealand has broad categories such as 'The Arts' and 'Social Science'. Singapore lists 'Health' and 'Physical education' separately while New Zealand puts them together. In both cases, these lists are just ways of setting out broad entitlements for children and of defining a rounded curriculum. In neither country are schools required to arrange the curriculum in these ways.

The 'Cambridge Primary Review' (Alexander 2009) recommended that there should be eight 'domains' in the primary curriculum. It chose the name 'domain' in preference to existing alternatives such as subject or 'area of learning' 'so as to allow them to be considered without preconception'. Alexander saw each of the eight domains as equally important and defined by 'coherence, integrity and an essential core of knowledge, skill and/or enquiry'.

At the same time, the Rose Review was proposing six 'areas of learning'. Neither system was greatly different, as seen in Table 7.1.

Rose did not include religious education because English law says this cannot be part of the national curriculum (it is not compulsory because everyone has the right to opt out). Apart from that, they are broadly similar, although the details may vary.

'Curriculum Matters'

In 1985, four years before the National Curriculum was introduced in England, HMI published their seminal 'Curriculum Matters' series (*The Curriculum from 5 to 16* – remembered by older members of the profession as the 'Raspberry Ripple' series, from the varying colour of the booklets). No book on curriculum design in England would be complete without reference to this work. It may seem long ago, so must be hopelessly out of date, and an odd reference in a book talking about a 21st century curriculum. However, the series was uncannily prescient, and its principles can be seen in play around the world in some of the most progressive and successful curricula today, such as those above (do they still read 'Curriculum Matters' in Singapore?) The one country where the series seems to have had least influence is in England itself.

In this series, HMI listed nine 'Areas of Learning' *'which should feature in a rounded education'*. These were:

- Aesthetic and creative
- Linguistic and literary
- Mathematical
- Moral
- Physical

- Scientific

- Spiritual

- Technological

Apart from science being separate from technology, this is very similar to the Alexander and Rose lists (did they read 'Curriculum Matters'?)

The important issue for curriculum design is how these various subject areas or domains fit together. HMI stressed that:

> [t]hese are not suggested as discrete elements to be taught separately and in isolation from one another. They constitute a planning and analytical tool. Nor are they equated with particular subjects (for example, a pupil may gain scientific or mathematical experience from art, and aesthetic experience from mathematics) although inevitably individual subjects contribute more to some areas than to others. Issues such as environmental education and preparation for the world of work are features of all or several of the areas, although the emphasis and nature of such work will differ from one area to another.

HMI were writing for the secondary as well as the primary curriculum, so their perception of areas of learning that transcend subjects was quite radical as well as visionary.

It encourages the curriculum designer to look at the range of subjects set out in a national curriculum as colours on an artist's palette. The colours are all set out separately but can be combined together to create a wide variety of pictures. The colours on the palette are at one level the different subjects, but at another level they are different aspects within a subject: shades of the same colour, as it were. The curriculum designer's skill is to make use of all these shades and colours to make a curriculum picture that is coherent, meaningful, engaging and worthwhile. In reality, the designer paints a series of pictures from the same palette, so the overall curriculum could be seen as a gallery. We might even make our way around the gallery by different routes.

We are now getting closer to Carla Rinaldi's vision of an 'arena of opportunities'.

What if we prefer some other country's areas of learning?

As most countries allow or encourage schools to arrange learning in different ways, the fact that they may be grouped differently is not an issue. The fact that a subject is not included in a national curriculum need not be an issue either; many English primary schools add other subjects, such as philosophy or a foreign language. The presence of a subject that you would prefer not to be there is more of an issue because there is a statutory obligation to teach it. However, as we pointed out in Chapter 2, there is considerable flexibility to cover aspects of the curriculum in depth or not as the school sees fit. There remains an overall obligation to make the curriculum balanced and coherent, but no one would want an unbalanced or incoherent curriculum anyway.

The real question is about how we decide which bits of the subjects to focus on, and in which order we introduce things within a subject. This is the second key question of curriculum design: How do we organise learning?

Subject disciplines

We suggested that there are three key reasons why subject disciplines are important. They represent:

- bodies of accumulated knowledge;
- structures for understanding that knowledge;
- systems of finding new knowledge within those structures.

These categories take us back to the three forms of learning in Chapter 1: knowledge, understanding and skills. These are the three aspects that distinguish one subject from another. It is not just the content of the knowledge (this often overlaps); it is also the way that knowledge is structured into understanding and the methodologies used within the subject. Together, these are the 'disciplines'.

Many years ago, R. S. Peters and P. H. Hirst (1971) suggested that what distinguished one subject from another was the way in which the truth of a proposition is established. For example, the truth of the proposition that 'metals expand when heated' can be established by a series of experiments within a scientific methodology. But the methods needed to establish that 'the invention of the bicycle was responsible for changing patterns of marriage' comprise a different (historical) set again. Peters' logic brought him to eight subjects – they were not the same as our English National Curriculum subjects, but were close to HMI's nine areas.

There are many other practical or theoretical ways of arranging learning such as Phoenix's 'Realms of Meaning' (1986) or Anderson and Krathwohl's 'Taxonomy for Learning, Teaching and Assessing' (2001), which point to other groupings. This is why there is no international consensus about what the subjects are or should be, or where one ends and another begins. For example, in terms of the English National Curriculum, the children looking in rock pools on the beach were studying Geography when they found out how the pools were formed, but Science when they found out what lived inside them. In Singapore, they would be doing Science all the time, because both life and the erosion of rocks are included in that subject. Does it matter? Is it not more important that children should be finding out about the world around them rather than arguing about which piece of learning goes where?

Although there may be disagreement about where lines are drawn and what goes where, there is a wide consensus that what is important to a subject is more than the knowledge content. There are systems and structures of thought that define how we understand a subject area, there are the specific methodologies that are used within the subject, and there is the range of information that has been accumulated by people working within that subject.

Subject knowledge

It is impossible to pass on all the knowledge within a subject to primary children (or any aged children if it comes to that. Even university professors can no longer know all their subjects – especially as the sum total of human knowledge is said to be doubling every four years. The minute you know everything, you've been left behind).

So it is necessary to **select** from within the established body of knowledge. There are four bases on which to make this selection:

- the inherent logic of the subject content
- the nature of the subject
- to establish a breadth of learning
- its application to a wider understanding

The inherent logic

This is the system most widely used for deciding what order things should be learned, and is based on the logical and practical notion that some things need to be learned in order that other things might be learned later. For example, in Maths it is logical and practical to learn to add up before one learns long multiplication. In fact, it would be impossible to do it the other way round. In Geography one would learn about erosion and about the hardness of different rocks before one learned about differential erosion.

This works for linear and logical subjects like Maths but does not always apply so easily to other subjects. Nor does it apply so easily to the way in which the human brain functions and children actually learn. In the geography example above, it is quite possible to reverse the logical order and first take the children to visit the Clifton Gorge in Bristol, and by seeing this example of differential erosion then to learn about how rivers cut valleys and about the hardness of different rocks. Many young Bristolians have learned about differential erosion in this seemingly illogical way!

Our human logic runs in a linear direction while our brain functions holistically. This was one of the key problems with the 'National Strategies for Literacy and Numeracy' in England. They set learning out perfectly logically in flawless sequences that would clearly all come together in the end. Unfortunately it all too often did not come together in the end because children do not always learn as logically as we would like.

This is not to say that the logic and practicality should be ignored, for it must be observed where we have evidence of its effectiveness. But it is to say that it cannot be the only way of deciding which pieces from the vast array of information within a subject area should be included in the primary curriculum. Having applied the logic we shall still need a further organiser, and that is to select the information to be included on the basis of its effectiveness in promoting a better overall understanding.

Subject differences

Not all subjects work in the same way in this respect. In the present English National Curriculum, in subjects such as Maths and Science there is a greater amount of knowledge 'content' than in subjects such as Art or PE, where the Programmes of Study are composed almost entirely of skills. Subjects such as History and Geography fall somewhere in the middle, being mainly skills but with some required 'content'. Within the knowledge content itself there are three key considerations for the curriculum designer:

- some aspects such as 'Ancient Rome' in History might be seen as 'one-offs': something for children to study once during a key stage;
- some aspects such as 'Electricity' in science might profitably be studied more than once during a key stage, once at a early level of making a circuit, and later a higher level of varying current through a circuit;
- some aspects, such as, say, writing reports in English need to be practised every year, and even many times a year, at increasing levels of difficulty.

All of the 'knowledge content' falls into one or other category, and it is a key aspect of the curriculum designer's role to decide which should be which. The distinction is not always between one subject and another, but also within subjects. For example, while electricity may appear several times across the primary curriculum, other aspects, such as 'parts of the body' might need to appear once only. The same is true of mathematics where aspects of number work need frequent practice.

Most of the Programmes of Study for English fall into the category of needing to appear every year. The National Literacy Strategy tried to split aspects up, but this was neither the original intention of the National Curriculum, nor the best way of learning things. The present Programmes of Study for English set out mainly skills, and then a short 'Breadth of Study' section. There is no suggestion that this range be taught discretely. For each of the three aspects (Speaking and Listening, Reading and Writing) the Breadth of Study suggests that the children be taught the range of 'knowledge, skills and understanding' through a wide range of types of communication, literature and writing. The list is there to ensure breadth in the children's experiences of reading, writing and communicating. It was never intended that children would study each type of literature separately or even 'study' them at all in the academic way prescribed by the National Strategies. The idea was to ensure some breadth to the books, styles and authors that a child would come across. Through reading that range, a child would acquire the skills and understanding of reading.

It would be a poor curriculum that enabled a child to attain a high level of reading ability, but had not introduced them to a wide range of authors. This brings us to a further consideration of the knowledge content.

Breadth of learning

It would be quite feasible in History for a child to spend all of the primary stage studying the Victorian period at increasing levels of difficulty. They could develop high level historical skills, and great depth of knowledge of the period. This is often what students do at university. However, it would mean that children would reach the age of 11 with a very poor general knowledge of history. They would also lack some historical understanding because they could not relate the Victorian period to any other or to the great sweep of history. Therefore they could not make judgements about, for example, what was unusual or significant about the period.

A primary school curriculum that taught children about only one period of history would, anyway, not be regarded as particularly broad, balanced, rounded or worthwhile. We would all expect well-educated 11-year-olds to have a certain breadth of knowledge as well as having skills and competencies. The problem comes when we try to make a list of all the things that an 11-year-old should know. This cannot be done in detail, and consensus at the level of detail is impossible to attain. However, there is a consensus that there should be some breadth and the national curriculum of each country attempts to provide this sort of breadth.

At the school level, the ensuring of this breadth is a key aspect of curriculum design. But the breadth needs to be ensured over the whole primary stage, and so does not necessarily tell us which aspects should come when. This is when we need to look at other factors.

The application to a wider understanding

The basis of this selection is the range of information that will make it most easy for a child to grasp the key elements of the subject and give them sufficient information to begin to use its methodologies. The selection is made with these key elements in mind, so to make the selection, we need to look at these key elements first. They are usually seen as Key Concepts and Key Skills.

There are two types of Key Skills: those that apply only in one subject are (Key Subject Skills) and those that apply across the subject areas (Key Generic Skills). Although they apply to all subject areas, the Key Generic Skills apply differently in each, and this is how an Area of Learning can be defined.

Key Concepts and Key Subject Skills

Key Concepts

These represent the key structural understandings of the subject discipline. If a young person understood these, then they would understand the essence of a subject. For example, a Key Concept of Geography might be that 'the landscape that we see was not always like this, it is the result of natural forces acting on it over time'. This concept is not readily apparent to young children. They typically imagine that hills and valleys were always there and were made that way. Once they have grasped the concept, they begin to see the world in a different way. They are also ready to apply this to other areas and ask questions about how cliffs or plateaux or deserts were formed.

Another Key Concept of Geography might be that 'the way people live is affected by the landscape they live in'. Again, this might not be readily apparent to a young child, but once they realise it, they begin to see the world differently. The key is how we get children to understand these concepts. Merely telling them is seldom enough.

Before we had a national curriculum, visitors to English primary schools were often puzzled by the fact that we spent time teaching young children (infants as they then were) about the people we then called Eskimos and now refer to as Inuit. Visitors objected that there are very few of these people in the world and you are unlikely ever to meet one so why spend time studying them. However, a very important principle of curriculum design is involved. If you want to get a 5-year-old child to understand the Key Concept 'that landscape impacts on lifestyle', then there would be little point in showing them a French or German family and trying to contrast their lifestyle with ours. There are differences, but they are too subtle for a 5-year-old to grasp.

So we show them an Inuit, with an igloo, a spear, a husky dog and sled and wearing a furry hood. This may be a simplification, but it makes the point to a young mind. If you live in a frozen landscape with no trees, you make your house of ice, and your transport is a sled. We select the example that best illustrates our key concept.

This remains a key precept of curriculum design.

Do you remember the children investigating the mystery of the parish register in Chapter 4? The Key Concept there was that 'new technology impacts on how we live'. We could explore this concept in any number of historical periods (and should do so) and look at things like the invention of the plough or the cannon or printing and see the huge impact these had. In doing this we are not just teaching children random bits of information, or even chronologically arranged bits of information – we are helping them to understand something really important about the flow of history and how things come about. If we explore this concept in the context of the Victorians we then need to select from the whole range of information about that period, and choose those bits that best illustrate the concept; in this case, the invention of the bicycle and the expansion of the rail network.

By focusing on the Key Concept, we do not need to teach the children every possible thing about the Victorians. We do not need to find out about boys sweeping chimneys nor do we need to colour in pictures of Victorian ladies' dresses. We choose only those aspects that best illustrate the concept.

If you are wondering what the Key Concepts are, you will find some set out in the English Secondary National Curriculum under that title. They are not in the present Primary National Curriculum, but some were set out in the Rose Review and many schools are finding these helpful.

So a key step in curriculum design is to clarify as a nation, or, failing that, as a school, what are the Key Concepts that we want our children to have grasped within this subject by the age of 11. You could start with the Rose Review or the secondary Programmes of Study, but then apply your own thoughts. You could start from scratch and list your own. Some Key Concepts for different subject areas are set out at the back of this book, but they are not definitive. Everyone needs to work through these for themselves.

To start with the Key Concepts is to start at the centre of Sinek's golden circles. These are the 'Why?': the reason why we are studying a subject at all is so that the child can grasp the Key Concepts. Once we are clear about this, the 'What?' of which bits of information to select fall into place. The other clarifying factor is the Key Subject Skills.

Key Subject Skills

There are two distinct approaches to this around the world. One approach is to consider those skills which might apply in different ways in different subjects. The other is to look at skills that would be employed in that subject only, and to select those that are 'key' in the sense that they are essential to that subject's discipline.

It turns out that there are few key skills that are peculiar to only one subject. Physical skills such as running or jumping might be examples of PE skills that occur in no other subject. Map reading sounds Geography-specific until you think about the interpretation of historical maps, or those showing climate change or the distribution of plants in science.

There are subject specific skills such as manipulating a paint brush in Art, or sawing wood in D&T, but it is usually argued that the 'Key' skill here is actually the development of physical control and this applies across all subjects where physical performance is required.

If we look, for example, at the present Programmes of Study for Art, as described in Figure 7.5, we find little that is specific to that subject:

And so it goes on; you can look for yourself in the Handbook. The final four words in the box come closest to being art-specific, but could easily be design and technology or ICT as well.

This is the case in the English Secondary National Curriculum which sets out 'Key Processes'. (A process is a sequence of skills, and most of the processes in the secondary curriculum are actually skills rather than processes, so for our purposes we shall call them 'Key Skills'.) Nearly all of these are general in their nature. For example, the three Key Skills for History are given as shown in Figure 7.6.

Programme of study for art and design at key Stage 1

"Exploring and developing ideas:
a) record from first-hand observation, experience and imagination, and explore ideas
b) ask and answer questions about the various starting points for their work, and develop their ideas

Investigating and making art, craft and design:

a) investigate the possibilities of a range of materials and processes
b) try out tools and techniques, and apply these to materials and processes including drawings
c) represent observations, ideas and feelings, and design, and make images and artefacts"

Figure 7.5 Programmes of Study for Art

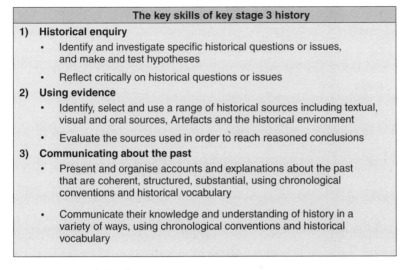

The key skills of key stage 3 history
1) **Historical enquiry**
• Identify and investigate specific historical questions or issues, and make and test hypotheses
• Reflect critically on historical questions or issues
2) **Using evidence**
• Identify, select and use a range of historical sources including textual, visual and oral sources, Artefacts and the historical environment
• Evaluate the sources used in order to reach reasoned conclusions
3) **Communicating about the past**
• Present and organise accounts and explanations about the past that are coherent, structured, substantial, using chronological conventions and historical vocabulary
• Communicate their knowledge and understanding of history in a variety of ways, using chronological conventions and historical vocabulary

Figure 7.6 the Key Skills of Key Stage 3 History

If you took out the words 'historical' and 'about the past', these skills could be applied to almost any subject. However, they would be applied differently in other subjects; what counts as evidence changes, as do the lines of reasoning used to reach conclusions, and how hypotheses can be tested. The conventions and vocabulary of communication also change: a scientific report is couched in different terms from an historical one. Children need to learn about these differences; they are part of being inducted into the subject disciplines.

Areas of learning

This brings us back to the notion of Areas of Learning explored earlier in the chapter, because the notion comes from the application of skills and the sharing of Key Concepts. The Area of Learning is defined as one in which skills are applied similarly and where the same Key Concepts apply across the area. This makes an Area of Learning much more than a 'bag of subjects', and more like the HMI definition of areas.

For example, most countries list 'Social Studies' within their primary school curriculum. The focus is on human beings, and how they live together now and did so in the past. This might include History, Citizenship and parts of Geography, and is why the physical aspects of geography are usually located in Science. But as the area is not defined as a list of subjects, it could equally include aspects of psychology, sociology, economics, politics and philosophy. The focus is on understanding the area rather than on subject content.

Defining the subject areas

The importance of the generic Key Skills is that they apply in every subject area, but are applied differently in each area. It is this difference in application that defines the area. For example, the way you would investigate in Science is different from a historical investigation where an experiment cannot be set up. In the Arts or Mathematics it would be different again. But investigation is an essential skill in each area.

To turn this round the other way, all things that can be investigated by scientific methods can be seen as falling within the area of science. Things that need to be investigated through the methodologies of social science fall into social studies. It is similar in the Arts or literature. In this interpretation, it is not the *content* that defines the subject area, but the methodologies that are applied within in it. This is why many countries, for example, put the study of rocks and erosion in science. Geography is seen as the application of social science methodologies and so is alongside history and economics in the area of Social Studies.

An example of the way the process (five Key Skills equal one process) impacts on curriculum design in the primary school would be a child who has made an animated film and wants to compose some sad music to go with it. They might investigate by listening to some pieces of music to work out what made them sad. They would analyse and synthesise by looking for the significant elements of the music – tempo, chords, key? Then they would 'create and develop' by composing some music of their own. Before they used it in their film, they might check that it is perceived as sad by other people. This is evaluation. In the Arts, the film itself will be the communication to others.

Solving a problem in mathematics would involve the same process, but it would be applied differently. The 'create and develop' might be the trying of different solutions. The evaluation would involve mathematical proof, and the communication might take the form of a mathematical equation.

Children need to be inducted into the appropriate ways to apply and develop these skills in different contexts.

So the set of five Key Skills can be seen as both a comprehensive set of operating skills, and also as a way of defining subject areas.

There is no absolutely right or wrong list of skills, many lists are in use around the world, and each list seems to have a fervent set of adherents. The skills are not really discrete anyway, but blend and overlap. It is seldom possible to apply only one skill at a time. Most situations require the application of several at once. For example, the children on the beach at the beginning of this chapter were investigating rockpools, but inevitably were analysing the information they were acquiring, beginning to synthesise this ('There are fish, shellfish and plants') and communicate it ('Look what we've found!'). Later they developed their ideas, evaluated those that were most significant and created a website to communicate their findings in more formal ways.

The key to curriculum design is to remember the reason for the importance of the skills, and so answer Sinek's 'Why?' The reason is that we want to equip the children with the skills and competencies they need in order to explore the world, and navigate themselves around the sets of accumulated human knowledge and experience. This may be a national list. It may be the national list amended, or a list from elsewhere. Schools across the world show that what is important is not which list you choose, but that skills are built into design. It is the way in which they impact on learning that is important.

This is what we look at in the next chapter.

8

How do Key Concepts and Key Skills impact on learning?

Persuasive Citizens

A group of Victorian parliamentarians, top-hatted and stern of face, is confronting a group of citizens who are energetically concerned about the plight of young children being employed in factories. The citizens make emotional appeals about cruelty and rights, but the parliamentarians seem unmoved. They do agree, however, to return in five days and see if the citizens can come up with any persuasive arguments for changing the law.

This is Monday morning in a Year 6 class and the parliamentarians are parents and governors, suitably attired. The citizens are the children, who really do seem energetically concerned about the lives of their historical peers. The parliamentarians will return on Friday, so the children have one week to find persuasive arguments.

They recognise that they will need facts and figures to persuade and so set about finding out about how many children were employed doing what and at what age; how many were killed and injured, what they were paid and how long they worked in what conditions. With all this information, they also recognised that they needed to set it out coherently and persuasively. On Wednesday, their teacher showed them six bullet points that help you be persuasive. The children pounced on these, and used them in their work.

The bullet points came, of course, from the National Literacy Strategy, but what an effective way to introduce them when the children had a real need to be persuasive, a real audience to persuade and the information already at their finger-tips.

The Parliamentarians returned on Friday, but defeated the young citizens who then demanded a rematch the following week. The teacher did not tell them this was not possible because History was now over, but allowed the work to flow. The result was a victory for persuasive citizens and, as we all know, the Factory Acts were brought in.

You will, no doubt have recognised the Key Concepts and Key Skills being developed by these young citizens. One Key Concept is that there are reasons for changes that happen within historical periods. There are Key Skills about investigation to find the information, and communication to persuade the parliamentarians. All these are being developed (once again!) in the context of the Victorians.

The design triangle again

The operation of the skills within a subject is very similar to the way generic skills operate inside 'triangles'. This time it is, in a sense, a small triangle within the subject box, as shown in Figure 8.1. The three points of the triangle are: Subject range and content, Key Concept and Key Skill.

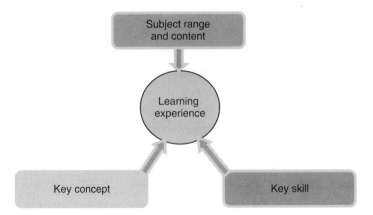

Figure 8.1 The subject triangle . In the example above, the subject was the Victorians, the Key Concept that 'there are reasons for changes within a period', and the Key Skills were investigation and communication. The design triangle, therefore, looked like the one in Figure 8.2

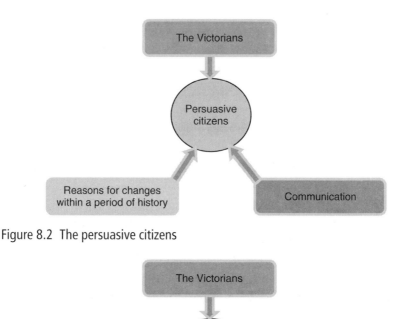

Figure 8.2 The persuasive citizens

Figure 8.3 The parish register, again

If in your class, children were already good at communicating, but you wanted to develop their investigative and analytical skills then the persuasive citizens learning experience would not work because it does not really focus on the problem-solving aspect of investigation. So what could we design instead? What would combine the Victorians, the concept of change and the need to solve problems through investigation?

Do you remember the Mystery of the Parish Register in Chapter 4? The conjunction of the Key Concept and the Key Skill in the context of the Victorians exactly fits the bill (see Figure 8.3).

If we were to make a change to any of the boxes in the triangle, then the central experience would be different. For example, if we still wanted to

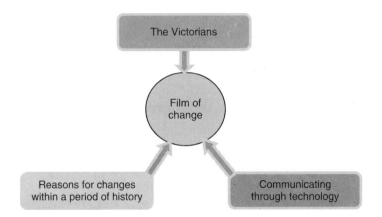

Figure 8.4 Film of change

work within the context of the Victorians, and still wanted to illustrate the same concept of change, but wanted a focus on communicating through a range of technology, it would change again (see Figure 8.4). What experience could you develop here?

One answer would be to ask the children to work in groups to make a film to illustrate how their own locality changed during the Victorian period. Where this has been done in schools, children have investigated the changes and worked out ways of illustrating these in film. Some have used a map from 1840 and made it fade into a map from 1900 showing how much bigger the town became. Some have animated this to show railways and roads snaking outwards and green spaces being progressively built over. Some have shown a series of photographs with a calendar flicking over. Their creativity is endless. Many have added soundtracks of appropriate music, and when they can find no suitable recordings, they have sung their own songs and made up their own accompaniment. They usually provide a voice-over that explains the changes that unfold during the film.

In each of these three examples, a key concept of history is rooted in a particular aspect while pupils also develop key historical skills. The key element of curriculum design is to select in each case the information that best illustrates the Key Concept and that gives scope for the development of the Key Skills. When the skill focus changed from investigation to communication, so the selection changed from the impact of bicycles on marriage to the plight of children employed in factories. Making this selection is the essence of the curriculum designer's art (or is it a science?)

Chapter 4 pointed out that linking skills and subjects enhanced learning rather than detracting from it. In the same way, making use of Key Concepts also enhances learning by focusing on the key understandings that promote deeper learning, rather than the amassing of information. The focus on Key Skills ensures that children are being inducted into the subject discipline, and not just looking at its surface content.

In terms of National Curriculum attainment levels, the pupils do well in all the examples. You know from Chapter 4 that Level 5 requires children to give historical explanations for changes. In each of the examples, change is the focus of the experience (of course, the reason it is a key concept is its importance to progress) and the explanation flows from the investigation or the need to communicate. So, high standards are not being compromised in an approach that values subject skills.

Does this approach only apply to History and the Victorians?

Perhaps we have overdone the Victorians, but the idea was to explore the impact of making one change only. We did look at Science in Chapter 4! So, let's look at Geography and turn this round. We'll start with the design triangle, and then think of the experience – as we would in the design process.

See if you can supply experiences for the following scenarios.

Scenario 1

The geographical context is Rivers. The Key Concept is that although there is variation in physical phenomena, there is a pattern to these things. The Key Skill that you want to develop in your class is communication in its widest sense (see Figure 8.5).

Suggestion 1

What have you thought up for this? What would link an exploration of patterns in the context of rivers with the skill of communication? First, we need

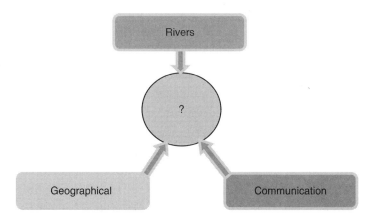

Figure 8.5 Designing for rivers

to be clear what the patterns might be. One way of looking at this is that all rivers conform to a similar profile in that they begin high in a hill as a spring or a pool, start off small, steep and fast-flowing, going over waterfalls, get wider and slower and finally meander to the sea. They carve out valleys and gorges. Along the way, people build settlements and bridges, and sometimes flood defences.

How could we illustrate this pattern? One school in Lancashire in England took its children out with digital cameras to follow the pathway of their local river (conveniently short from source to mouth!) and record its changing path. Back in school they searched the internet for film of other rivers and found good footage of the Mississippi in its various stages. They then put the bits of footage together to bring out the fact that although the two rivers are very different indeed in terms of size, length and the terrain they flow though, they both start high as a spring, then have a steep and narrow, fast-flowing section before widening out and eventually meandering to the sea. Along the way there are settlements, bridges and flood defences.

Conscious of the demands of subject-appropriate communication, the teacher ensured that the children made use of maps and contour lines as well as film to illustrate the various sections of the rivers. They made a papier-mâché model of their own river from an Ordnance Survey map, and panned the camera down to get the aerial view they could not capture in real life. They kept refining their film and wanted to add a suitable soundtrack and voice-over. This led to them exploring the different sorts of blues music that is associated with different parts of the Mississippi. The teacher did not say, 'You can't do that because this is geography, and we only do music on Thursdays.'

In another school using the same scenario, they could not find any suitable footage on the net, so they contacted schools along the Mississippi and asked if they would send footage and other materials. The result was a joint website illustrating similarities, differences and patterns. Other schools joined from other countries and the learning became richer and richer.

In terms of Geography attainment, Level 3 requires pupils to compare and contrast places they study, Level 4 to identify geographical patterns, and Level 5 to give geographical explanations for those patterns. The children certainly attained Level 4, and in most cases Level 5. So, again, the high standards 'flow' from the approach. Because the Key Concept is geographical patterns, it is hard to avoid Level 4 attainment. Yet how many times do we see children spending weeks studying rivers without identifying, let alone explaining any patterns that might be evident.

Scenario 2

The geographical context stays as Rivers. The Key Concept is still patterns. This time, the children are already good at communication, so you want to focus on problem solving. What experience could you devise for this? See Figure 8.6.

Suggestion 2

Have you solved this problem? There are many things that could be done. One school altered the scale, equipped the children with wellington boots, took them to a local stream and set them problems to solve. Why is the water moving faster here than there? Why is there a small sandbank here? How could we prove that the sand is being eroded from the other bank? How could we measure the width of the steam where it is too deep to get across?

The first problem involved deep paddling as well as deep learning. They were in groups and left to find their own solutions, but found it convenient to confer between groups. The children threw in sticks and timed their

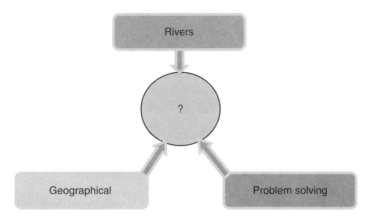

Figure 8.6 Problem solving in the context of rivers

passage to establish the speed at various different points, but noticed that the water tended to be shallow where it was most rapid. They then tried to calculate the volume passing by trying to find the area of a horizontal section of stream at the rapid and slow points. They did this by measuring the depth of water with a stick at regular intervals across the stream. They put this on squared paper and worked out the area. With the area and the speed they worked out how much water was passing each minute. This is easy to write but very difficult and very wet to do. The excitement was immense when they worked out that the amount of water passing per minute is constant. A large volume moving slowly is the same as a small volume moving quickly. They had established a principle, and come to a profound understanding of a geographical phenomenon. 'Of course,' one said, 'it has to be the same, or where would all the water go?' Wherever be the river, from local stream to the Mississippi, the principle is the same. And the reason? Because it is the same amount of water that is flowing, and it has to go somewhere.

Back in school, the children were keen to look at examples of large rivers and see how they conformed to basically the same pattern as the local stream: eroding the outside of bends where the water is rapid, depositing on the inside and building sandbanks. More excitement when aerial shots of the Mississippi reveal the same phenomenon, and the children know why. So, Level 5 attainment in terms of Geography again, but just think of the Maths and the problem solving as well.

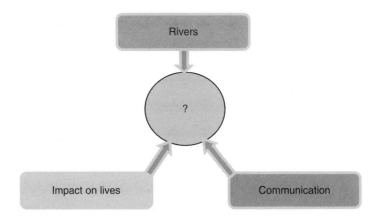

Figure 8.7 Communication in the context of rivers

Scenario 3

The geographical context stays as Rivers. The Key Concept is the way that rivers impact on the lives of people living alongside them. The Key Skill goes back to communication. What experience could you devise here? See Figure 8.7.

Suggestion 3

A school in Leeds looked at life along its local river and contrasted it with the River Indus. Many of the school's pupils were of Pakistani heritage, and the school was keen to bridge the cultural gap and increase international understanding, so this fitted well with wider goals. They visited the River Aire and found out about the Indus from books, the internet and from relatives living there whom they emailed and who sent photographs and video clips. Many of the children had visited Pakistan and could give first-hand accounts. Two questions arose: how can we sort out all the information, and how can we present it?

The answer to the first was to sort similarities and differences (Level 3) and to look at the ways in which, wherever you are, the river impacts on your life (Level 4). To present two different lifestyles while communicating the impact of the river was difficult, and it was the children themselves who came up with the idea of performing plays that portrayed life by the river in the two countries.

Capitalising on unexpected opportunities and unintended consequences

Unexpected opportunities

The above scenarios seem to suggest that that all these experiences are designed by the teacher or the school and are played out according the pre-ordained design. In reality, things seldom run so smoothly, especially when dealing with children. The best laid plans are apt to go astray. Children come up with their own ideas, and often these are better than the ideas we have ourselves. In the above examples, it was the children who suggested performing a play, and it was the children who suggested contacting schools in the USA when they could find no suitable footage on the net. These opened up whole avenues of learning covering wide areas of the curriculum that the school took full advantage of, even though they could not have been part of the original designs.

We have all been in these situations: the children are excited, we can see the possibilities for learning, but we are worried about being distracted and diverted. We feel the pressure of having all these other things to cover, so can't give time to follow these opportunities.

The answer is to see the unexpected opportunities as the chance to 'cover' other aspects of the curriculum we were intending to do later. In that way, we are not distracted from our core purpose, but are achieving the same ends through different means. When the children making the film about the two rivers wanted to add a music soundtrack, the teacher saw it as an opportunity to cover some of the music she had intended to do later in the year. So she is not being distracted or being taken up some blind alley; she is flexibly responding to a developing situation to maximise learning.

Now, you may be saying that it was highly unlikely that she ever intended to study the variations of Blues music in the Mississippi basin. And you would be right. But one of the Key Concepts in Music is that *'people from different times and cultures have used the arts in different ways to express ideas and communicate meaning'*. This Key Concept can just as easily be illustrated by American Blues as it can by the Indian Ragas or South American flute music that the teacher originally had in mind. So, although she may be deviating from the detail, she is not deviating from the essence.

She can do this because she has a clear understanding of the essence of the learning involved, and understands WHY she wanted the children to learn particular things about music. The 'Why' here is the Key Concept. She is more concerned about the 'Why' than about the 'What', and that is why she can be flexible with confidence.

In terms of Sinek's golden circles, she is operating in the centre circle. What she is changing is in the outer circle. It is when we think only of the outer circle that we become inflexible. We think that we must adhere to teaching about Indian Music, because we have forgotten why we were doing it in the first place. Once we remember why, we realise that we can just as easily illustrate the Key Concept with American Blues. Of course, we might even deepen learning later on by looking at Indian music as well, and by then we shall be adding to an already developed concept, so shall probably need to spend less time than we envisaged.

We talked about curriculum designers being like artists with a palette of colours. We are now looking at teachers as taking this to the next stage and 'designing on their feet'. This is where the science may well become an art. The teacher is more like the jazz musician extemporising, picking up on what has been played, catching the mood, and taking the music in a new direction, but one that stays true to the theme and the key and the mood.

Unintended consequences

As well as situations developing in ways we had not intended or envisaged, there is also the tendency of learning experiences to have unintended consequences. Children do not always learn what we expect, and often learn other things instead, or as well. We need to take account of these unintended consequences – both negative and positive. If children do not learn what we intend, then we need to take steps to arrange for them to learn these things at some later stage. If they learn things that we had not intended, then we need to take account of this too and amend the future programme to take account of the fact that some aspects will now be unnecessary.

To allow all this to happen, we need a framework for extemporising. Something that will give us the confidence to be flexible in the knowledge that a series of learning experiences that have been allowed to develop in different ways will still add up to a coherent and worthwhile curriculum.

A coherent set of experiences

The same imperative also pertains to the designing of a series of learning experiences. Even if we keep to our design, how do we ensure that they are more than a series of one-off experiences that may be valuable individually, but may not add up in the end to a coherent set, and a worthwhile curriculum?

This is the next chapter.

9

Putting it all together: a framework of expectations

The Demolition Company

The Demolition Company has a contract to demolish a disused factory chimney in Manchester and dispose of the bricks in an ecologically friendly way. To win the tender, it had to work out how many bricks were in the chimney, how much rubble would be produced, where suitable disposal sites could be found, and how many lorry trips would be involved over what distance. It had to consider the impact of dust and noise on local residents, and the environmental impact of dumping on various sites. It worked out the likely number of bricks that might be reclaimed and what the resale price might be. With all this information it was able to submit a tender price.

And now, a week into the contract, an email arrives saying that the selected disposal site is no longer available and the closest alternative is 10 miles farther away. What will be the percentage difference to the costs?

No one in the Company seems to know how to work out percentages, and faced with having to reply to the email, go to their teacher for help. You knew, of course, that the Demolition Company is run by children. In this case it is a virtual company run by a Year 4 class in a primary school where nearly all learning is through a 'Mantle of the Expert' approach where children assume a role and play out an extended role-play scenario.

The teacher at first affects surprise that the children do not know how to work out percentages. Then she says, 'Come here and I'll show you how to do them'. The children eagerly cluster round and immediately rush off to put their new learning to practical use.

Of course, it is the teacher herself who sent the email in the first place. She sent it because she knew that these children needed to learn this aspect of mathematics, partly because it is an important part of mathematics, and also because it is a requirement of the National Curriculum. What she has done is to create a situation where children have a real need to learn about percentages, a real audience and situation in which to practise this new skill, and a considerable emotional commitment to learning percentages at this point.

The whole curriculum in this school is designed in this way. All day every day from Reception to Year 6 is extended role-play. The specific learning the children need is fed into the scenarios by the teachers. The advantages are illustrated in the percentages example: emotional commitment, and urgent need for the learning and a 'real' audience and situation in which to apply the new learning. If you have never tried this approach, or tried it once and said, 'Never again!' you might see that the disadvantages are: having to think up such scenarios and then to keep them going! Interestingly, the people who practise this approach are usually fervent in their support of it and claim that it's not difficult at all. It is mentioned here not to advocate it as an approach, but to see what sort of structure is needed to underpin it.

It is a good example of the need for a structure, because it is probably the ultimate in flexible approaches. There are two parts to this. First, the scenarios are devised by the teachers who explore between themselves the possibilities the situations might offer. They then list the learning that might fit within it; so they start with a rough idea of the learning the scenario might bring about. In the example of the demolition company, the teachers saw the opportunities for mathematics calculation about the number of bricks in a chimney and that this would involve calculating a circumference from a diameter. They also saw the possibilities for science and citizenship in environmental impact studies about disposal. They saw possibilities for English in writing to local residents to warn them of disruption and holding local meetings to hear complaints (parent volunteers took the role of aggrieved local residents). So it was seen as a rich source of learning.

The second phase is the actual development of the scenario day by day with the children. It is here that the children impact on the scenario themselves and take it in directions the teacher might not have envisaged. This may close down some learning opportunities, but open up others, so curriculum design needs to be flexible and responsive.

There is even flexibility about how long a scenario is kept going 'as long as the children keep learning from it. Sometimes we abandon them before we had expected, but often they go on all term or longer. So long as there is a sense of excitement and opportunities for the learning we want, then we keep it going. It soon becomes obvious when a scenario has had its day.'

The key to curriculum design is when the school refers to, 'the learning we want'. This is not just a vague aspiration, but a set of carefully structured year-by-year learning expectations. Most schools that take a flexible approach use a very similar system. They need to have a clear set of objectives so that they are able to select from them in the confidence that the flexible approach will still enable the learning to be rounded, coherent and worthwhile.

The secret to this is that the objectives are about what the children need to learn, not what they will do to learn these things. They are mainly the key concepts and skills in the centre of the golden circles.

What does this 'Framework of Learning Expectations' look like?

The learning expectations need to take account of the various aspects we have considered so far; both leaves and roots:

- Key skills
- Personal development
- 3C competencies
- Subject areas

Schools using this 'Framework of Expectations' approach generally set out expectations for each year group or stage of development within these headings. The expectations may vary from year to year with different cohorts, and will be revised in the light of the actual learning that takes place, but will provide a useful overall framework. To see how this works we need to look at how the Framework can be set out and constructed.

Year groups or stages?

The reason that most schools sort their Frameworks out by year group is because that is how their classes and teaching are organised. In a typical English primary school, children stay with the same class for the whole year and are taught almost entirely by one teacher. It is therefore logical as well as convenient to think about the curriculum in this way. If your school has mixed-age classes, then you probably have a different way of organising the curriculum, such as a two-year rolling programme. Of course, the Framework would need to reflect your pattern of organisation.

There is no suggestion in this organisational approach that every child in a year group (and even less so in a mixed-aged group) will be at the same stage of learning. However, it is not unusual for all children in the class to be following the same topic at the same time, such as Ancient Rome or electricity. Teachers will need to interpret the broad structure in the light of the actual children in their class. In some years, it might be possible to exceed the usual expectations, or there might be a need to start at a lower point. In some years, the range might be wider than in other years. What is important is to give some structure to the organising of the curriculum if we are to enable flexibility of design to meet children's interests and needs. The structure is provided by the four elements outlined above, and we shall take these one at a time below.

Key skills

We have not yet considered how these might develop as the child grows older. One way is to do this in stages (Levels) or roughly by Year Group. To take the latter course is not to suggest that the development always happens in exact year group stages, or that every child in a year group will develop at exactly the same rate. But, if the classes in a school are arranged in year groups, then this makes some sort of sense. The Rose Review used three stages (Early, Middle and Later) that roughly equated to Years 1–2, 3–4 and 5–6, but which allowed for differential progress.

There is no right or wrong here, and different schools have made a success of both of the approaches. For schools with mixed-age classes, the year-group framework would not be particularly useful. In other circumstances, it might work well. So it is really up to schools which approach they adopt. The important thing is to have some sort of framework around which teachers can design experiences and construct learning: a structure that allows teachers to extemporise.

Let us use levels of attainment to illustrate the point. The levels could relate to the National Curriculum levels, or could be stages. If we apply this to the first of the Key Skills – investigation – we would want to get some sense of how children would progress in terms of this skill. There might be two parts to investigation: finding things out, and making increasingly refined sense of the things they discover, as listed in Table 9.1.

In terms of evaluation, the sequence might be as shown in Table 9.2.

These are couched in very general terms; too general, you may think, to be of use. However, most schools find that they can work comfortably at this level and keep their eye on the 'big picture' of progress rather than get lost in the detail. Some schools might want to refine lists like this and make them

Table 9.1 Investigation

Level 1	Observe things around them and recognise simple features
Level 2	Describe and order their observations and make suggestions about investigating
Level 3	Make comparisons and contrasts, and develop their own ideas for investigating
Level 4	Plan investigations, make generalisations and detect patterns,
Level 5	Plan more complex investigations and give explanations for detected patterns

Table 9.2 Evaluation

Level 1	Recognise simple features
Level 2	Suggest improvement to their own and other's work
Level 3	Modify and refine their own and other's work
Level 4	Analyse work in relation to its intentions and use
Level 5	Use the analysis to develop and improve work

more detailed. The most useful way of doing this is to relate them to the actual investigations in which the children will engage.

For example, what would you expect the children on the beach to be doing when they investigate rockpools? If they are in Years 1 or 2, then we might expect them to be observing things and be putting those observations into order. They should be able to answer questions such as, 'What different things live in each pool?' and 'Can we sort them into groups?'

By Years 3 or 4, we might expect them to be making comparisons and contrasts. Are their different types of things living in larger pools than in smaller ones? Higher up the beach or closer to the sea? What other comparisons could we make? How could we be sure we are accurate in our conclusions?

By Years 5 or 6 the children might be able to generalise their findings: the larger the pool, the larger the shellfish, or sea anemones are only in the pools closest to the sea. And they should be able to suggest some explanations for these: there is more food in the larger pools so the shellfish tend to grow larger.

The level of definition of the skill may be very general, but it can be applied specifically and makes a significant difference in terms of progression. In fact it brings rigour to the learning. Just think how children might explore rockpools without this framework in mind. How many would be prompted to the intellectual level of generalising and explaining? How many 11-year-olds would still be identifying and listing? Setting out a pattern of progression in these general terms is extremely valuable, because the effectiveness comes from the general level and its application in different situations.

The benefit of keeping to the more general terms is that they have application across the areas of learning, and as we said in Chapter 6, it is this difference in application that defines the area. The same system of defining levels or stage of progression also operates within the other skills.

Personal development

These can be also set out in terms of progressive expectations. If we take the 'team work' or 'collaboration skill' from the previous examples that might be seen as shown in Table 9.3.

Again, these are broad criteria that need to be interpreted within the actual experiences in question. In the parish register example, the Year 6

Table 9.3 Collaboration

Collaboration	
Level 1	Take turns and share
Level 2	Work co-operatively on a task with a classmate
Level 3	Work as part of a larger group with a defined role
Level 4	Define and agree different roles within a group. Recognise what makes the team operate effectively
Level 5	Play different roles within a team to expedite its work. Give constructive feedback to other team members

children might be jointly planning their investigation and splitting up the tasks to get the job done quicker. They would meet to discuss their findings and agree their interpretations of the data. They would hear different points of view and come to reasoned conclusions (just like staff meetings!).

3C competencies

In Chapter 2 we looked at the advantages of identifying 'essential' or 'functional' elements of literacy, numeracy and ICT: those elements that are applied and unlock learning in other areas. They are competencies because they involve both knowledge and skills and also require appropriate attitudes. As these competencies are most usually used in other contexts, it is much more efficient to learn and develop them in those contexts. This does not mean that they would never be taught separately, but that the main development would take place in context.

There is hardly any context in which some aspect of 'essential' literacy, numeracy or ICT would not apply. It is hard to learn without at the very least some listening or reading, so some aspect is within almost every learning experience. What is important is to take this inevitable part of the experience into an intended part.

Progression is linked to the present attainment of the children in the class. In the Demolition Company example, percentages were fed into the experience because that is an aspect of maths that is part of the overall programme. It might be the case that a different class or group would have a different need. This might have been identified through the school's assessment procedures or an analysis of SATs. It might be that the reason SAT scores are not higher is poor performance in data analysis. So how can we improve this aspect? We can arrange extra data-analysis lessons, or we can feed this learning into other learning experiences. Could we get the children on the beach to tabulate and graph the distribution of life in the rockpools? Could they analyse the market variations in fish prices after speaking to the fisherman? Could the Demolition Company graph the cost variation in taking the rubble farther to a cheaper disposal site? Could the Fruit Machine Company look back at their records and look at seasonal fluctuations in profit margins?

If the children in question were already good at data-handling, but needed extra practice with, say, measurement, then the design would be amended. The children on the beach could be calculating the tidal range, the volume of water in the pools, the speed of tidal change or the varying size of seaweed at different points on the beach or life in the rockpools. The Demolition Company was, anyway, involved in working out the dimensions of the chimney and size of bricks to calculate the number. They were also calculating lorry-load sizes and distances travelled.

This is curriculum design responding to immediate need. It is also the injection of rigour and high standards into what was once seen as a 'woolly' topic approach. We have noted before that competencies developed in context are more likely to be able to be used in context than those learned in isolation, so there is a further advantage to this approach.

The final part of the equation is the contexts in which all the skills and competencies are developed.

Subject areas

In one sense, this is what traditional curriculum plans do already: long-term plans chop up the programmes of study into annual and termly 'chunks'. Traditional medium-term plans arrange these into lessons. Even in the most creative and flexible approaches to curriculum design, there will always be a need for some sort of overall allocation of these aspects of learning. There must be some system for ensuring that children do not study the same aspect six times and miss out the others. There is also a need for schools to assure themselves that the whole six- or seven-year experience adds up to a broad and balanced curriculum and coherent whole.

With the Personal Development, Key Skills and 3C Competencies, it was possible to split these into stages or levels rather than year groups. This is because different children within a class are likely to be working at different levels or stages. However, with the 'content' elements of a subject it is much more likely that the whole class will be working together on the same aspect, such as Ancient Egypt in history, electricity in science or a village study in geography.

The way this works varies from subject to subject. Some subjects, such as Maths and Science have much more specific 'content' than subjects such as Art or even English, but there needs to be some sort of allocation to avoid gaps and repetitions, but this need not be extensive. For example, in the present English National Curriculum there are six specific periods to be studied in history and five topics in geography during Key Stage 2, so the task of allocating these is not too onerous.

To a great extent, then, the subject element of the framework is very similar to the traditional long-term curriculum plan. However, we need to shift the emphasis in the way this is done. The key to successful design is to look not just at the list of content, but at the Key Concepts and Key Skills and then let teachers decide what aspects of the content would best illustrate these.

Move away from the 'What?'

The difference between curriculum planning and curriculum design is in the way these are allocated. The shift is from the outer circle of, 'What' to the inner circle of 'Why'. For example, many long-term plans for history at Key Stage 1 list 'Florence Nightingale' and 'The Victorian Seaside'. The reason why these have been chosen is that we want children to 'find out about the lives of significant people from the past' and to 'explore how people's ways of life change over time'. If we list these deeper reasons, rather than the content title, in our overall annual programme, then two advantages accrue. First, we are more likely to focus on the deeper learning rather than the surface topic. Second, we leave the teacher more room to design an experience that will fit with the wider flow of learning.

Florence Nightingale might not fit with other developments in the term (the extension of work on the beach and the lighthouse might make Grace Darling more appropriate), so it would be better to take some other person from history and not study Florence Nightingale at all. This would not matter if we remember why we put her in the curriculum in the first place.

Similarly, at another school, it might be more appropriate to look at some other aspect of change other than the seaside. This does not deviate from our core purpose, which was to explore an aspect of how the past was different. The key is to pick an aspect that will make sense to the children and which will resonate with their lives.

There will remain some other aspects of subjects that will need to be allocated to avoid duplication or being missed. For example, at some point in Science children need to learn about electrical circuits and the effect of varying current through a circuit. Is this something that children need to meet or explore every year from Year 1 to Year 6, gradually deepening their understanding, or is it something that can be met once only? Or is it a wider topic that that can be broken down into smaller elements that can be part of the programme for each year group? These are decisions for the school to take, depending on the level of understanding of the children concerned.

Move away from fixed time allocations

What we do not need to do at this overall stage is to allocate times. It is often our own time allocations that impose the rigidity that we seek to escape. When teachers come to the medium- and short-term stages, they quite understandably tend to fill up the time that has been allocated. Having filled it up, they then worry if they find it difficult to get through it all. If they were given the learning objective to complete at some time during the year, then they could include it in their design at the most appropriate time. They could also decide how long to allocate. It would also leave them flexible to decide that the children have now learned this so we can move on to something else – even though we have not yet had the half-term break.

Does this apply to English and maths?

We have become conditioned in our approach to these two subjects by the National Strategies. It has become almost impossible to imagine how anyone managed to learn to read or to add up before these Strategies came into primary education and broke learning into separate strands. Many schools have moved on from an over-structured approach, but this does not mean that there is no need for any structure at all. Chapters 5 and 6 were all about ensuring that learning experiences are designed to focus on exactly the piece of learning that our children need at that time. This will come from a combination of the framework and the Levels. English and maths are somewhat different in the way they come into curriculum design, and both are different when we apply the 3C Competencies.

Both subjects are affected by taking out 'essential literacy and numeracy' as part of the 3C Competencies, and building these in across the curriculum. The parts of English and maths that are left tend to be those parts that we have always tended to approach through whole class experiences anyway. The 'essential' parts of the subjects would be in the framework for the 3C Competencies we discussed above. This cannot be allocated in advance to whole classes as it depends upon the children's level of progress at the time. Teachers would work from the overall framework to design the learning that was relevant at the time; just as percentages were built into the demolition company experience for those children who were ready for this.

Once we have taken out the 'essential' elements, the rest of the subject can be treated as we treat other subjects. In Chapter 11, we shall look at the impact this might have on SAT scores (it's positive – or we wouldn't be talking about it!)

How do we do all this?

There are three ways of doing this. First, by starting afresh and going back to our aims and intentions and the National Curriculum Programmes of Study. This involves throwing out our existing plans and, even more difficult, letting go of the pre-existing ideas that J. M. Keynes said were so hard to relinquish. Few schools are willing to take such a radical approach, and many worry that they would be throwing out much that is good along with the bad. However, if you are really keen, and really dissatisfied with what goes on now, then it has to be the best way forward.

The second way of approaching this is to take your present long-term plans and ask some rigorous questions about each element. The key issue is whether we are achieving the outcomes that we want. Which of our aims are we meeting; which are we missing? There is an assumption that we are not

Table 9.4 Analysis of long-term plans

1	Why is this element included? What is the underlying learning intention? Can we list this intention instead?
2	Is this learning intention really appropriate for children of this age?
3	Does this piece of learning really need to be here? Is it a requirement of the National Curriculum? Is it required in this form?
4	Can we take it out, or do we want to do it anyway?
5	Is there anything missing? What should we include that is not in our present curriculum?
6	When we analyse the overall programme in terms of learning intention rather than content, is it still coherent and sufficient?
7	If we were starting again, would we set it all out like this?

meeting all our aims, because, if we were, we would not be making wholesale changes to the curriculum! However, you are unlikely to be missing them all and there will be successful parts of the curriculum that you will want to preserve. Armed with this analysis, we then need to look at the present plans in detail, as explained in Table 9.4.

At the end of this exercise, you are likely to have an outline that will facilitate design rather than planning, that will focus teachers on the key learning involved rather than covering content, and that will give the flexibility needed to ensure that learning meets the children's needs.

The third way of changing your curriculum would be to buy a complete curriculum 'off the shelf', or download one from the web. No doubt there are some excellent curricula for sale, but they were not written for your school or with your pupils in mind. If you have read this far in this book, you are probably someone who would rather design your own and make it work in your situation. Whatever you start with, the National Curriculum or someone else's interpretation of it, you will need to adapt it to your circumstances and so go through most of the same procedures.

However radical a review you undertake, the key is to come up with a framework that is based on learning expectations rather than content, and which gives teachers flexibility to design learning experiences within these contexts that give good grounding in the subject areas while building personal development, key skills and the development of 3C competencies.

Looking back as well as looking forward

The framework operates in two ways. First, it is the palette from which the teacher draws the colours to paint the curriculum picture. Second, it is the record of what has been learned. In designing the learning experience, the teacher will make a record of those aspects she intends to include. But as the experience evolves and concludes, the teacher will revise that record in the light of:

- Intended aspects that were not actually included after all;
- Aspects that were included, but were not originally intended;
- Aspects that were included but which the children, or some groups of children, did not actually learn.

This record then becomes the basis for planning the next experience: including the things left out, bringing in new things and going over old things that were not fully learned. This developing design gives the flexibility to respond to assessment information; it is 'Assessment for Learning' in action. It can only be done because there is a clear structure of learning expectations.

Drawing up the structure of learning expectations

If you have never worked in this way, you might still be wondering how to go about drawing up the expectation for each stage or year group. Or you might at this stage think it is really straightforward, and it will not be until you start that the difficulties become apparent. You might also be wondering why this book does not just tell you what the structure should be – especially after you have paid so much for it! The answer is, of course, that to be effective the structure must be yours and reflect your circumstances and understandings. However, there are some suggestions on the related website. Please adapt these rather than using them as they are!

In reality, it is not until you start to *use* the structure that it will become really clear what it should look like in detail. At that point, you will no doubt go back to the structure and amend it.

Putting it all together

Early chapters looked at triangle models as ways of seeing how various elements of design fit together. We have now extended the range of elements to four so we need a process model that takes account of these:

- Key skills
- Personal development
- 3C competencies
- Subject areas.

All of these feed into the wider map of the curriculum that we considered in Chapter 1. The curriculum was seen as more than lessons, so in design we can consider routines, events and out of hours learning as well. This made up a map of the different types of learning.

Each of the four elements could contribute to any or all of the types of learning, as shown in Figure 9.1.

In the example of the parish register, the pupils might be seen as engaged in a series of subject-focused lessons. The design of these lessons included:

- **Subject area**: History, the Victorians
- **Personal development**: working in teams
- **Key skills**: investigation and problem solving
- **3C competencies**: use reference texts, analyse data

This can be shown as in Figure 9.2.

The beach example might be seen as a local study, but it still has the four elements feeding in.

- **Subject area**: Science: life and living things
- **Personal development**: working in teams

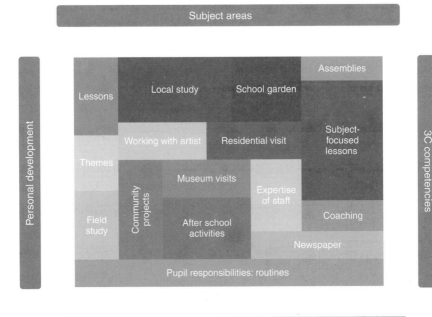

Figure 9.1 Overall model

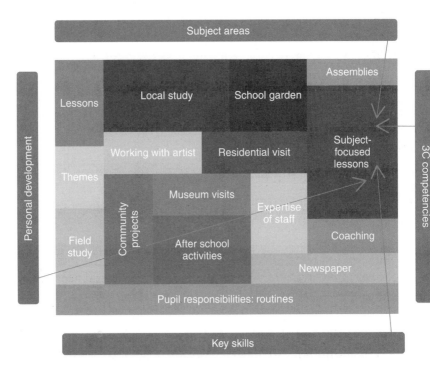

Figure 9.2 The parish register in the overall model

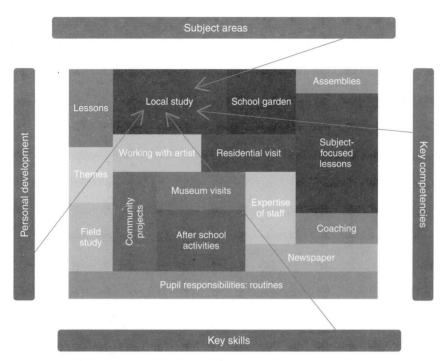

Figure 9.3 The beach example in the overall model

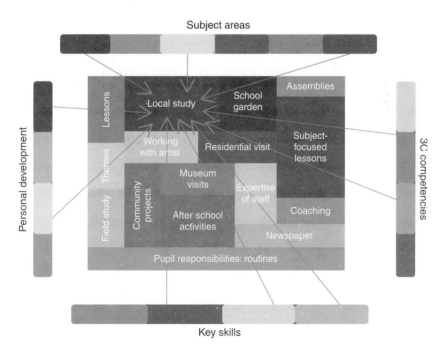

Figure 9.4 The refined model

- **Key skills**: investigation

- **3C competencies**: measurement

This can be shown as in Figure 9.3.

We could refine the model and indicate that the subject areas and skills are, in fact, each made up of different areas and skills, and that more than one of these is likely to be involved at any one time. Back on the beach, the children were involved in Science and Geography for the subject areas and in investigation, evaluation and communication from the key skills. So the model should look more like the one shown in Figure 9.4.

At this point, the model is already complex enough without adding extra elements, but if you have been following so far, then you will no doubt recognise that, in fact, every one of the four 'outside' elements is capable of contributing to every one of the curriculum boxes. We could draw arrows from all the outside boxes to all the inside ones, and each would be valid.

This direction of the arrows is seen, of course, from the curriculum designer's point of view. In reality, and from the child's perspective, it is the experience that contributes to the learning of the skill, competency, subject understanding or aspect of development. So the arrows should really go the other way, as we discussed in Chapter 3, and as shown in Figure 9.5.

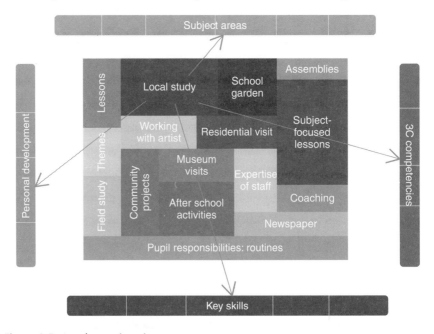

Figure 9.5 An alternative view

We design the learning experience by considering which learning elements we need to include in order to meet the children's needs. At the end of the experience, we look at the process in terms of the contribution of the experience to the children's learning, and so reverse the arrows. At this point the Framework becomes a structure for recording what has been learned.

The process in action

The contents of the four outside boxes (Subject Areas, Key Skills, Personal Development and 3C Competencies) form the long-term structure of learning expectations that has been drawn up for each year group or class.

The process of design is to draw in these threads and weave a rich tapestry of learning; or to dip the curriculum design paint brush into each of the four outside palettes to paint the curriculum picture; or some other high-flown metaphor that you might prefer. The teacher draws upon the learning expectations and combines them into a series of experiences that are lessons, routines, events or a combination of these.

As the term and year progress, the teacher checks the structure to see what has already been included so far, and what has been learned. This informs the continuing process of design by noting what has been learned, and indicating what needs to be learned next.

When the process works well, the clear structure of expectations frees the teacher to design experiences that are truly creative.

10 A creative curriculum

Animated Science

Children in a group of rural primary schools became very keen on making animated films. At first they were really pleased with the films; any bit of animation was exciting and they were proud that they could do it. But with time, they could see that their results were not as good as Wallace and Grommit and they became dissatisfied. What could they do to make their films better? They studied Nick Park's work and other animations but could not work out how to do it. How do they do it at Ardman? The teachers recognised that they did not have the skills to help the pupils, and so decided to bring in outside help from a firm of animators.

Because each school was small, they decided to put the children together from Years 5 and 6 for a day-long course from the professionals. This was where the interesting arrangement came in. Discussion with the professionals disclosed that there were three key parts to the course: animating models, filming techniques, and lighting and editing. Each element would really take all day. So the children were split into three groups on the day and each did one of the three courses. The courses were held in three different schools.

When they came back to their own school, the children were put in teams of three – with one member from each course. So it was only between them that they knew how to make a film, and each had a unique contribution to make. These were real teams, not three people trying to do the same thing at the same time.

The task set to each was to make an animated film to show the Year 3 class how shadows change with the movement of the light source. So the teams had to make sure they understood the science, think how to convey the key points to younger children, decide how to sequence the films, come up with novel and engaging approaches, and then apply all they had found out about animating models, lighting, filming and editing. This they did with enthusiasm. There were some extremely good films about creatures frightened by their own shadows, shadows that grew huge and grotesque when the light source was close, shadows that disappeared at noon, and shadows that seem to acquire a life of their own. All were greatly enjoyed by the intended audience, and were a great hit on the joint website. The film makers agreed that the key was the lighting which gave the animations a 3D quality that had been missing before, even though their models were in 3D.

What is a creative curriculum?

Many schools in England say they are following a 'creative curriculum', but the term seems to cover a wide range of approaches. When asked, 'Does this mean that the curriculum helps children to become creative, or that the curriculum is designed creatively?' many schools answer, 'Both, really.' Unfortunately, in some cases, it is neither.

If a creative curriculum is one that takes a creative approach to design that puts things together in different ways that constructs learning experiences which were not immediately obvious, then that is what the whole of this book has been about so far. But it has been about creativity with a purpose. This creative curriculum is not about doing things differently just for the sake of being different. It is about finding better ways of enabling children to learn (Craft, Cremin and Burnard 2008).

The opposite of a 'creative curriculum' might be a 'prosaic curriculum' or a 'ploddingly obvious' curriculum. This is the curriculum that lists the things that children need to learn and sets out the detailed order in which these things will be taught, with little thought to why we want children to learn these things or how they might learn them best (remember Sinek?).

It often focuses on a narrow range of measurable attainment, and often ignores the more difficult to assess learning of skills, competencies, values, attitudes and overall understandings. It also takes little account of the connections between one thing and another: either between one subject and another, or between subjects and skills or even the connection between learning and life. The neatness and logic of laying out the curriculum in a well-ordered and carefully planned way, looks really good in the curriculum plans, and in the chart on the headteacher's wall, and in the brochure and website. Unfortunately such neatness and logic does not accord with the way in which children learn (Goswami 2008). Nor does a detailed, six-year plan give scope to take account of what children might or might not have learned as they go along, what their changing interests may be, what circumstances might alter or what new opportunities might arise. Some people feel that a six-year plan is somewhat uninspiring in that it lays out for a 4-year-old what they will be doing in the summer term when they are 11. That is the equivalent to being 30 years old and having it pre-ordained what you will be doing in the summer when you are 75. Some might find it comforting, but most would find it dispiriting. And is education not about awakening curiosity, widening horizons, stimulating the imagination, opening up different pathways? How is this consistent with a rigid six-year plan?

The 'plodding curriculum' tends to be linear, yet learning is more like the neural network itself. Learning is seldom linear, and is richest when it is most connected. The 'plodding curriculum' is about planning, while the creative curriculum is about design. So if the 'creative curriculum' is to be effective, it must be about finding better ways of putting learning together in ways that avoid the pitfalls of the plodding curriculum. It cannot be about doing things differently, but not making learning any more effective. It must ensure that the curriculum

- is based on the agreed principles and values;
- builds on what children have already learned;
- makes learning comprehensible;
- is relevant to children's lives and circumstances;
- makes links between subjects and with skills;
- responds to developing opportunities;
- provides intellectual challenge.

A creative curriculum is not one that will take children away from what they need to learn. It is not just a matter of taking children to the woods, picking flowers and dancing round a tree. But, of course, it could be that if picking flowers and dancing promoted the learning that was intended. For example, the Year 3 and 4 children in the example below were taken to a wood, and while they were there, they did pick some flowers. And, because they came from a very urban environment, part of the value was to experience being in a wood and to appreciate the beauty, the atmosphere, the sights, the sounds and the smells. But the focus was an aspect of the English National Curriculum that everyone does at some time: study a contrasting locality.

Case Study: A Contrasting Locality

When the children came back from the wood, they talked about all the ways in which it was different from their urban surroundings. The absence of traffic and roadsigns was high on their list. They also noticed that there were no seagulls in the woods, yet they were common visitors to their school playground in their coastal town. In most schools, the lesson would then become one of writing a list of similarities and differences.

In this case, the children were invited to suggest how they could express these differences, and they came up with the idea of making roadsigns and seagulls and taking them up to the wood. This was not in the teacher's plan, but the making of the signs and gulls became part of Art and D&T. The children looked at their local road signs and discussed how to make them. They even contacted the Forestry Commission to get permission to put the signs around the wood.

The class went back to the woods with their assemblage of signs. They saw the leaflets of woodland walks in the visitors' centre, and agreed with the Forestry Commission that they would produce their own leaflet for an 'Urban Walk'. This meant more unplanned work photographing the signs and designing their own leaflet in the style of the official ones. The children printed these at school and they were put in the visitors' centre.

Back in school, they wondered how they could show the contrast the other way. There was little enthusiasm for making sufficient model trees to plant a forest in the playground, but they did plant some trees. They also imagined what it would be like for some mythical 'Woodland Folk' to come to their town and experience the traffic. This resulted in a masked play that they performed for parents.

When they eventually went back to the wood to remove their now somewhat soggy roadsigns, they were shown the visitors' book where people had written, 'We did enjoy the urban trail'. Nothing could surpass the swelling pride in each of those children on reading these words.

This is a creative approach to a very common aspect of the curriculum, but did it enable the children to learn what is normally expected? Comparing and contrasting is the Level 3 expectation appropriate for children of this age, but it is probably the quality that has been enhanced here. Everyone can intellectualise about the similarities and differences between one location and another. But to see the roadsign in the wood is to go beyond an intellectual understanding and to actually 'feel' that the sign is wrong there. This is taking the learning of geography to a depth of understanding not normally reached.

Standards and a creative curriculum

There is a worry that a creative approach to the curriculum will sacrifice a focus on 'standards', by which people mainly mean standards of attainment in English and Maths as measured by national tests. There is no reason why this should be the case. In the examples given so far, all the schools achieved high standards in national tests *because* they took creative approaches, not in spite of them. If the key to a creative approach is to make learning more effective, then children will learn more this way. If they learn more, then they will do better in tests. But, through a creative curriculum, not only will the children learn enough to do better in tests, they will learn much more than this. They will learn about the connections between aspects of subjects, they will acquire learning and personal skills, they will develop certain attitudes and values, and become more self-confident and independent. They may even learn to be more creative.

Where does animated science fit with this?

This may be seen as a creative approach to curriculum design in that it is more than the common approach of a set of separate science lessons on light and shadow, together with some ICT lessons on stop-frame video and editing. The idea of building on the children's interest, and linking science and ICT with the film, creating a known audience and using outside trainers was beyond the ordinary.

Just think about the amount of learning that took place here. There is all the social learning that went with attending a course (like an adult) in another school and working alongside strangers. There is the finding out about science in order to explain it to someone else. There is working in a team where each member has her or his own unique contribution and also needs to listen to the others. There is working out good ideas for the film and then using all the ICT and communication techniques that had just been learned to make it.

So is this an example of an experience that encourages or develops creativity? What is creativity? Is it something that can be taught?

Will a creative curriculum make children more creative?

In his 1999 report on creativity in education, *All Our Futures*, Prof Ken Robinson, suggested that '*creativity always involves thinking or behaving imaginatively*'. This accords with most common sense understandings of creativity. It is about the imagination, thinking of new ideas, putting things together in different ways, thinking 'outside the box' or coming up with new ideas.

Robinson goes beyond this and says:

- First, creativity always involves thinking or behaving **imaginatively**.
- Second, overall, this imaginative activity is **purposeful**: that is, it is directed to achieving an objective.
- Third, these processes must generate something **original**.
- Fourth, the outcome must be of **value** in relation to the objective.

The notions of purpose and value do not always spring to mind along with imagination and originality when we think of creativity.

In their book *Creativity, Wisdom and Trusteeship* (2007) Professors Anna Craft, Howard Gardner and Guy Claxton took up this theme. They refer to the creative process as being a combination of:

- Convergent thinking
- Divergent thinking
- Practicality
- Social worth.

Craft et al. have taken Robinson's first point and seen the process as involving both convergent and divergent thinking. The other points about being purposeful or practical and about creativity having value or social worth are broadly the same. They all agree that creativity is more than 'novelty for novelty's sake'.

So how does this apply to primary children? Within this broad understanding of creativity the process might go something like this: Having made their animated films, the children want to add a musical soundtrack that will convey the sadness of losing your shadow. They decide to compose their own music, but how could they make it sad?

First, they might listen to some pieces of music that they see (or hear!) as sad and see if they can work out where the sadness resides: is it the tempo, the key, the chords or the sort of instruments? They then try out some ideas of their own, and check these with the others to see how they sound: 'Does this sound sad? How about this?'

This, of course, is the process of convergent thinking (investigating existing pieces of music), divergent thinking (developing your own ideas), and practicality (checking whether it really does sound sad). The social worth here will be in the enthusiastic reception the whole film receives from its audience.

This four-part process is very similar to the five key skills we have been using in this book:

- Investigation, analysis and synthesis (convergent thinking)
- Designing and developing (divergent thinking)
- Evaluation (establishing practicality)
- Communication (establishing social worth)

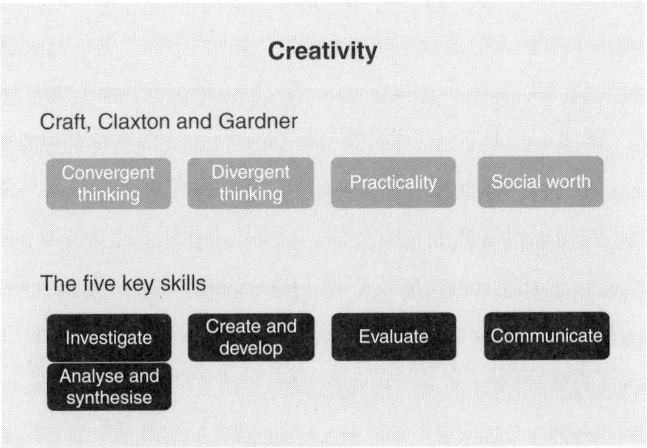

Figure 10.1 Creativity and the five key skills

You might object that communication does not really establish social worth, but it does put any creation into the social domain, and is probably the closest one can get within a primary school context (see Figure 10.1).

This analysis sees creativity as being more than novelty. Originality is a necessary but not sufficient condition of creativity. To encourage or develop this in children, they need scope and encouragement to exercise their imaginations and to come up with new ideas and approaches. They also need the discipline to ensure that these original ideas are also practical and of some value.

A dual approach

Creating opportunities

The first part of the approach is to design experiences in which children have scope to be creative. If these sorts of situations are new to them, then they will need time and encouragement. Ken Robinson argues that children are born creative but that they tend to lose the faculty along the way through lack of use. Children in the nursery seldom have problems with creative play, although there are some who have already started to lose the ability even at this age. This is why it is important for primary schools to keep these opportunities open; creativity is something you use or lose.

All of the experiences we have been talking about so far in this book would give opportunity for children to be creative. It does not have to be Art or Music, and the scope for creativity can be within structured boundaries. In fact, many children find it easiest to be creative when the boundaries are not too wide. The parish register children were creative in their approaches to solving the historical problems and adducing proof for their theories. The Fruit Machine children spent their lives thinking of new products, approaches and marketing ploys. The Demolition Company children were confronted daily with the need to come up with new ideas in response to an ever-changing situation. The 'roadsigns in the wood' children and the scientific animators were no less creative in their more artistic approaches. All of these experiences give scope for creativity.

Above all, children need *time* to develop creative ideas. Too often, children are rushed and have few opportunities to come back next day to have another go, or implement an idea that came to them overnight. Google gives its employees 20 per cent of their time to think up new ideas. That's a day every week away from any requirement to carry out directed work. There are rooms where they can sit and talk, sofas to sprawl on, equipment to try out ideas, colleagues to share ideas with. How much time do we give our children, and still expect them to be creative? What facilities and environments do we give them to encourage their creativity?

A Roman Helmet

A 9-year-old boy had written about a line and a half in his book, but was flexing his fingers and shaking his wrists as though in agony. 'My hand hurts after so much writing,' he announced, and left his seat to go over to a table where balloons were covered in papier mache. Here he set about completing the Roman helmet that he was constructing as part of a history unit.

'Whenever I get stuck with my writing,' he explained, 'I come over here and have a go at my Roman helmet. After a bit, I get a good idea about my writing and go back and get on.'

By the end of the afternoon, he had written over two pages of a rather good story and had almost completed his helmet.

Don't we all need a 'Roman helmet' to resort to when we are trying to be creative? The writing of this book has required countless stops to make coffee and look at the newspaper, but how often to we give children this flexibility? In how many schools would the Roman helmet boy have been told that he needed to finish his writing before he could get on with his helmet? But spending time on the helmet was exactly what he needed in order to get on with his writing. Creativity needs time, encouragement and also a flexible environment in which it can flourish.

The discipline of creativity

Although creativity and discipline may not seem to go together, alongside the opportunity must come the discipline. Children need to be encouraged to develop their imaginative ideas. Encouraged not to stop at the first idea, but to explore more; to check that the idea could work, to find out how it could work better and how it can be communicated to others.

Teachers often find that some children struggle to come up with new ideas; but all the more reason to help them to do so. Many children struggle with writing, so they are given extra help. It is worth remembering that the first part of the process is 'investigation': finding out what ideas other people have had. This starting point is often missed when we ask children to be creative, yet it is an essential start to the process. How many children have been asked to write a poem, when they have come across very few poems in their lives and sometimes have only the vaguest of notions of what they are for? This step is not there to encourage children to imitate other solutions, but to look at them for inspiration and guidance, and to help ensure the practicality and worth of ideas.

The divergent thinking stage is also a stage that needs a disciplined approach. Designing and developing does not mean accepting the first thought that come into your head, but considering a range and then working on them to make them right. Some children making an animated film were concerned that the movements of their plasticine figures did not look at all right. So they videoed themselves making the same movements and stop-framed the film to see the relative positions of their arms and legs through the sequence of movements. Armed with this information, they went back to their plasticine and made the movements look much better. This is all part of the creative process.

Such refinement is also part of the evaluation stage where the children ask, 'Is this working?', 'Does it fulfil the original intention', 'Is this what we wanted?' This is the practising and rehearsal, the editing and amending, the trying out and improving; the 95 per cent perspiration that needs to go with the 5 per cent inspiration.

Creating the creative curriculum

Of course, the same process applies to the curriculum designer trying to create a creative curriculum. Both inspiration and perspiration are needed. We need to look at what other people have done (and there are many examples in this book) and then apply the principles in our own situations. We need to develop and refine those ideas, and check that they work. And, like the children, the more we do this, the better we shall get at it.

And also like the children, it is better to work in groups. Most creative companies find that ideas come when people work together and spark off each other. So we must look at our curriculum planning meetings. For a start we could call them curriculum design meetings; that might go some way to seeing them as part of a creative exercise. Then we could focus on designing experiences that are exciting and inspiring for our children. This is a truly creative task.

If we already have the framework of learning expectations that we talked about in Chapter 8, we do not need to spend our time writing lists of all the things we want the children to learn; we have that already. Nor do we need to spend out time writing lists or spider diagrams of every possible thing a child could learn under a given heading in a period of half a term. What we need to do is to think of exciting experiences that will involve the expectations that have been set, and which will open up as many possibilities as possible. When our planning meetings become design meetings, then we are part way to creating creativity.

> **A Year 5/6 Design Meeting**
> The agreed focus was the Victorians, but the low-attaining class needed a great deal of practice with writing descriptions, in which their performance was poor. They also needed more practice with investigation and critical thinking, and in terms of personal skills they needed to work independently.

So the discussion was centred around the sort of experiences that would give opportunities for all these. Writing descriptions of pictures of Victorian life was dismissed as too boring. Bringing in Victorian artefacts for the children to describe was better but hardly riveting. And neither involves critical thinking. A treasure hunt round a museum with clues as to what to find would be better. And the children could be asked to write descriptions of exhibits and the other children would have to identify them from the description. This is getting better. They could even record the descriptions and the other children could listen on headphones like you really do in a museum (who reads in a museum?).

If they are given an exhibit each then looking at all the exhibits could add up to a whole picture of an aspect of Victorian life. The children would have to work out what the connection was between the exhibits. That would be the critical thinking element. The children could then weave all of these into a play or a film. That could be up to them to decide.

The next day, a teacher came up with yet another idea, 'Why don't we take them to (a Victorian house), and say that they are Victorian detectives investigating a murder. We could plant clues and they would have to find the clues, write descriptions of the rooms for their police reports, and work out what had happened.'

Once they started, the teachers became more and more enthusiastic about the project, thinking up scenarios and clues, suggesting which exhibits might link together. And when the project started, the children caught the teachers' enthusiasm. The creative process feeds off itself.

When curriculum design works at this level, learning becomes irresistible.

11 Making learning irresistible

Seeing Stars

Late at night in the middle of a wood, a group of 10-year-old children is lying on the ground looking up at the stars. Few of them have ever been in such darkness before. Away from the streetlamps of their home environment, and on a night with no moon, the darkness is palpable, and the excitement has been mounting as they walked through the wood by the light of their torches. Now they have turned off their torches and, looking up at the sky through the branches of the trees, they can see more stars than they have even seen before. The teacher does not have to say anything. The experience is enough in itself. The group falls silent.

The experience is part of the school's approach to developing writing skills while on a residential visit.

What example would you use to illustrate irresistible learning? Would it be a lesson, event, routine or something that happened out of hours? Would it be something wonderfully exciting, whizz-bang and totally out of the ordinary? Or would it be something simple and well crafted, or a combination of things? The phrase 'making learning irresistible' is frequently used by schools to denote an aspiration to design learning experiences so constructed that children could not help but learn, but most people think in terms of the excitement rather than the construction. What did the children learn in the wood? And what did it have to do with writing?

Many of the examples of learning experiences given so far in this book are of experiences that have some excitement, that are always engaging, but that also structure learning. The children solving the mystery of the parish register were engaged by the task, but it was so structured that they could not help but explore the reasons for a social change in Victorian times. The children putting roadsigns in the wood could not help explore the similarities and differences in the localities. Engagement is essential, excitement would be very helpful, but neither would be sufficient in itself if there was not some element of curriculum design that was structuring an experience in such a way that learning is inevitable.

In the example of the Demolition Company, the whole role-play scenario and the urgent email set up a real desire to learn about percentages. But there was also the element where the teacher explained percentages in such a clear and cogent way that the children were able to rush off and use them to answer the email. The other important part of the structure was that there was an immediate opportunity to use the skill in a practical situation for a 'real' audience. Part of the irresistibility was that the children did not only gain a theoretical understanding of percentages, they gained practical understanding.

The fact that we are trying to create 'irresistible learning' implies that there must be some other kind of learning – presumably 'resistible learning'. This must be learning that children can 'resist' in some way. So, what makes learning irresistible? Either the children choose not to resist, or could not resist even if they wanted to. This learning would be like eating an extra chocolate – 'I just couldn't resist!' So one way of seeking to identify the features of irresistibility would be to list the reasons why children might instead choose to resist. This has been carried out with countless children – asking the question both ways – and the list of reasons not to learn is always fairly similar:

- It's boring;
- I can't see the point;
- I can't understand it;
- It's too hard;
- I'm fed up with writing;
- No-one ever helps you.

Asking children what makes a good teacher comes up with a similar list (in reverse). Children often have a very good idea of what works for them. A good teacher:

- Makes it interesting for you;
- Explains things clearly;
- Listens to you and treats you with respect (doesn't get cross and shout);
- Helps you when you're stuck;
- Gives you time to finish.

The key to the children's analysis is that learning needs to be interesting, not just by being about something interesting, but also the way that learning unfolds and gives the children something interesting to do (usually other than to just listen and write). Children like to see the point of the learning; it has to have some relevance to them and their lives (Goswami & Bryant 2007). This is less important to younger children, and for older children there seems to be a trade-off between interest and need. If they see a real need to learn something then they seem willing to put up with less interest; if it is really exciting, then they don't need to see the point at all, because being excited is point enough. The interest needs to be linked to clear explanations. It is important that the learning takes place in a supportive environment; stress over not understanding things, getting things wrong and not having enough time is not conducive to learning.

A wider whole

Many aspects come together to make learning irresistible. Exciting experiences by themselves do not constitute irresistible learning, neither do cogent explanations that fail to interest the child. A visit to McDonalds will excite many children but will not, of itself, constitute irresistible learning. The most lucid explanation will not work with children who have fallen asleep through boredom.

So, there may be a number of factors in making learning irresistible, not just one magic key to unlock learning. These constitute the 'quality' aspect of curriculum design, as opposed to the 'functional' aspect. We may design experiences that will achieve our aims, but the question is how well they do so. We don't want to design learning experiences that are adequate, we want to design experiences that are compelling and make learning irresistible.

Of course, the nature of the irresistibility must depend upon the nature of the learning intended. Learning a skill such as handwriting might need a very different set of experiences from the development of caring attitudes towards wildlife, or the understanding of abstract concepts of equivalence in algebra. But although the cases are different, they have features in common.

Getting back to traditional methods

In his own engaging conference presentations, Trevor Hawes has suggested that if we want to make learning really engaging for children, then we must 'get back to traditional methods'. But he turns the clock a long way back to get to those methods. He points out that for most of human history we have learned from other members of the family or tribe. We learned things that were essential to our way of life: hunting, lighting fires, building shelters, cooking, how to store food and so on. We learned in practical ways by engaging in the actual tasks. We learned holistically without learning being broken down into discrete steps. Above all, we had a strong emotional commitment to learning. Our brains have evolved to learn in this way after thousands of years.

Learning in classrooms from strangers who are not part of our tribe (for the most part), while sitting with 30 other children of exactly our age and listening to the stranger talk is far from a traditional method of learning. It is, Hawes points out, a 'new-fangled experiment in learning that is not working out very well so far'.

The features that Hawes picks out as being part of the 'traditional methods' to which our brains are attuned are:

- Learning as a group experience;
- Relevance to the learner's life;
- Active involvement;
- Learning in a practical situation;
- A holistic approach;
- Emotional commitment to learning.

This is very similar to the set of features identified by the children themselves – perhaps it really is the way their brains have developed! But how do we build these features into our design?

Exciting children's imaginations

We would not be very ambitious about our curriculum if we seek merely to interest the children, or even to excite them. A visit to McDonalds can excite many children, but exciting their imaginations takes learning a step further. This does not have to be an exercise in fantasy, but could involve imagining different solutions to problems or ways of expressing things. The children making animated science films had their imaginations excited by the possibilities that the film course opened up. The children debating with the Victorian parliamentarians were excited by the prospect of the encounter. The more open-ended the experience we design, the more possibilities there are and the more scope for imaginative responses.

Irresistible learning is not a drudge. It finds ways of uplifting the spirit as well as the mind. It finds ways of making necessary practice enthralling. It excites children with the prospect of learning percentages, or with the arguments used by the Victorian factory reformers. It brings the parish register to life.

Fitting with how children learn

In Chapter 7, we looked at the different ways in which children learn knowledge, skills and understanding, so one key way of making the curriculum fit the way children learn is to take account of the type of learning involved. But we can go beyond this. There has been considerable progress in research into how the human brain functions, and there is a growing literature about the implications this research has for education and the curriculum (Katzir & Pare-Blagoev 2006, Immordino-Yang & Damasio 2007, Goswami 2008 and Wolfe 2010). Neurologists do not claim to know entirely how the learning process works, but some points have emerged, many of which seem to line up with professional wisdom:

- Learning involves the making of new connections in the neural pathways. These are physical changes made within the brain in response to external stimuli (seeing, hearing, feeling things etc.).

- This process is holistic rather than linear (there is not a single neural line that enables you to do long division).

- The wider the range of stimuli the greater the learning (listening is not always the best way of learning, especially for young children).

- The brain is capable of making hundreds of new connections every second.

- Skills learned in context are more likely to be able to be performed in that context.

- Emotional engagement (being interested, being excited, seeing the point) seems to help connections be formed.

- Stress gets in the way of learning.

Such considerations form the basis of most of the examples we have looked at through this book. Holistic learning with a range of stimuli, learning in context and strong emotional engagement have been features of experiences from the Fruit Machine Company to the children on the beach.

We know from much earlier writings on learning such as Vygostsky (1978) that children are active learners, not only in the physical sense, but in seeking to make meaning of new experiences. This is corroborated by more recent work such as Gardner 1999 and Goswami and Bryant 2007. Children need to be active rather than passive in their involvement in learning. They need to have something to do, something to explore or investigate or create. Listening is a way of absorbing some information, but it seldom leads to deeper understanding without more active engagement.

Fitting with childhood

The curriculum needs to prepare children for the future as adults, but it also needs to recognise that they are children in the present. We need to ask ourselves whether our curriculum really recognises that children are only 5 years old when they start primary education. What should children of this age really be doing? Playing? Taking part in a literacy hour? Are we rushing our children into adulthood without giving them time to be children first?

There is something universal about childhood, wherever you go in the world. If we do not tune our curriculum into that, it will fail.

Some schools have sought to address this by agreeing with parents and governors (and the children themselves) a 'Charter for Childhood' that lists all the things a child should have done by the age of 11. People list things like 'Walk along the beach barefoot and feel the sand between your toes', 'Go to a theatre' and 'Look after a pet'. The schools often talk to parents about what the school will do and what will be done from home. But the list can add to the joy of the curriculum.

Part of fitting with childhood is learning through play. This is not something to be left behind in the Nursery. It is a very effective way of learning. When adults get together on business courses, what do they do? Role-play. They learn by playing. Or they are put into teams and given problems to solve and scenarios to work through. Yet this form of learning sometimes disappears in the primary school. It is almost like an old-fashioned view of medicine: if it doesn't taste horrible, it can't be doing you any good; we can't have the children enjoying themselves, they've got far too much to learn.

The Northern Ireland 'Council for Curriculum, Examinations, and Assessment' (CCEA) puts the value of play clearly within its National Curriculum:

> Children learn best when all areas of an integrated, carefully planned, curriculum are implemented informally using methodologies that are interactive, practical and enjoyable. Children should have opportunities to experience much of their learning through well planned and challenging play. (CCEA 2003, p. 7)

Alongside considerations of play, comes meta-cognitive learning. There are certainly times when it is helpful to be aware of what we are learning and to think about how we are going about it. But there are also times when the sheer joy of finding things out should be allowed to take over. The more complex the situation, and the richer the learning, the less possible it is to be meta-cognitively aware of all that is going on. If the brain is making hundreds of new connections every minute, we cannot keep track of them all. We can be aware of some simple lines of superficial learning and keep track of that, but the complexity of deep learning will always elude our conscious minds.

Resonating with the children's own lives

For many children, what goes on in school bears little relation to their own lives or what goes on at home. Most seem to accept this parallel universe where values and concerns are so different, and even what counts as knowledge can also be different. They accept it, but the disjuncture impacts on their learning. If the curriculum does not connect with children's lives, it will leave them behind. We can end up with a curriculum for 6-year-olds about nouns, adjectives and phonemes, while the children's concerns are about their pet cat, their new shoes and their turn in the class shop. This is how we can end up treating 6-year-olds like medical students when they only need to be able to sort their heads from their heels.

On the other hand, the curriculum cannot merely wrap itself around the children's lives. It must take them places they have never been, and show them things they have never seen. It must widen their horizons and increase their realization of all the possibilities that are open to them. But the curriculum cannot do this if it left them behind at the very start.

Practical and firsthand

All of the examples we have looked at have been of children engaged in firsthand practical experiences. This does not mean that all learning experiences need to be like this; indeed, there were times within the examples when the children were looking things up on the internet or in books, or listening to experts on a course, or listening to explanations from their teacher. For learning to be irresistible, it does not have to be the same all the time. Modulation, variety and fitness for purpose are part of irresistibility. There will be times when children are sitting and listening to their teachers. There will also be opportunities for:

- open-ended situations where children co-operate with each other to solve problems;
- focused whole-class or group subject teaching;
- independent study;

- coaching and mentoring;
- time for reflection and consolidation.

The key is to ensure that the experience is appropriate to the intended learning.

Over the course of a learning experience, all the forms may come into play. Irresistibility is in the long-term and not just in the immediate.

Back to the wood

After the star-gazing experience, the children talked about their experience the next day. They had not attempted to write, or even to talk about writing whilst in the wood. So it was the next day that they discussed how to convey those feelings to others, and agreed that this depended on the medium and who the others might be. The immediate medium was the website which was updated each day of the residential visit to keep parents in touch. They were given the opportunity to write briefly or at length. The focus was firmly on the communication, not on the form. (They were not asked, 'What genre are we using?' nor 'Have you used adjectives and adverbs?') But behind even this lies an approach to writing through the school that has made learning to write well irresistible.

It is worth looking in a bit more detail at the wider context of making learning irresistible. The children in the wood are from a school with an average intake, but 95 per cent attain Level 5 in writing. The school had never followed the National Literacy Strategy, but they must have been doing something right! Their key phrase is 'Less is More', by which they mean that less writing means more quality and less teaching means more learning. You may have noticed that 'Teach less, learn more' is also a feature of Singapore's approach to curriculum design. So there might just be something to it!

'Less is More' – how does the school make the learning of writing irresistible?

Underpinning the stargazers' success in writing is the width of experiences that the school organises for the children, 'We need to give children something to write about.' It is not just the experience, but the talking about the experiences that equips children with the language they need for writing; during the discussions, adults model the appropriate vocabulary, structures and patterns of expression. The discussion also deepens children' understanding, and so enables them to marshal cogent arguments and write clear accounts. Models of good writing are also provided by reading good quality stories to the children and ensuring they have access to good quality language through books, tapes, CDs and other resources. Listening to a story is not something these children do when their work is finished; it is an important part of learning to write well.

Next comes a clear purpose and audience for writing. Writing is not just an academic exercise; it is an act of communication. 'We don't expect children to write all the time, or just for the sake of it. There has to be a purpose. So there is probably less writing going on than in most schools, and far less in exercise books, but when children do write they have something they really want to express, and a clear audience to express it to, and so a need to write well.'

The school uses a variety of ways for children to present their work, not just writing. These include film, drama, oral and multimedia presentations. The school finds that this widens children's abilities to express themselves and clarifies their understanding of the needs of communication. One example was the daily 'blog' posted on the school's website during the residential visit. This gave parents immediate access to their children's experiences and gave the children a real audience for their communication.

The school sees writing standards being enhanced by elements of the foundation stage approach being used through Key Stage 1 and into Key Stage 2; for example, there are role-play areas in all classrooms where children are encouraged to be creative in their approach and to speak and listen in a variety of situations. The school playground is equipped with a stage and children make use of this in breaks for impromptu drama and performances. The school finds that all of these activities and experiences feed into better writing. So there is less writing, but more ways of communicating and this has not detracted from writing standards, but has contributed to them.

Each class enjoys a rich diet of visits, visitors (such as local writers) and first-hand experiences. There is considerable flexibility to allow these experiences to be arranged because no class has a fixed timetable and so teachers are able to ensure that interests and valuable learning can be pursued. The school has found that less structure in the timetable allows a richer range of experiences to be arranged.

Underpinning the school's successful approach is the involvement of children in the life and work of the school, and the sense of ownership they have of the school and of their own learning. Children have considerable independence to shape their own learning, with discussions held at the beginning of new topics to decide on its direction. Enterprises have been set up and run by the children. Children are responsible for many of the routines of the school and the arranging of playground activities. In this sense there is more from the children and less from the teachers, but the impact is on the commitment of the children to learning and the confidence with which they approach it. It also means that active children have a wide range of experiences and a real desire to communicate to others. It is this that provides the foundation for their writing success, makes learning irresistible and makes attaining Level 5 almost inevitable!

Irresistible design

One of the features we have looked at in irresistible learning, and which is also used effectively to promote writing, is the linking of learning to the local context. The curriculum that does not connect with children's own lives and experience will be all too easy to resist. National expectations must be located firmly in local settings. This means not only the geographical locality of the school, but also the personal reality of the children.

We explore this further in the next chapter.

12 National expectations in a local setting

> **Cockles and Mussels**
>
> The seashore rocks are covered in shellfish, and the Year 1 children are absolutely fascinated by them. 'What are they?'; 'Look at his one'; 'There must be millions'. On finding that these shells are alive, the children are even more amazed.
>
> Yet these children live only five hundred metres from the shore, and knew nothing about it. Some had not even been there. The school had realised that some of the 11-year-olds had never been to the sea, even though they had lived so close all their lives, so a programme was started to set learning in the locality.
>
> The children found some loose rocks with barnacles attached and took them back to school. In the classroom the level of excitement was immense when they first saw the feeding 'fans' emerge to filter food from the water. So much life, so close, that they know nothing of – and such a thirst to find out more.

One of the effects of the National Curriculum in England has been a tendency to make learning experiences universal. All across the country, children are studying the Second World War or the Romans, the habitats of animals or the way to construct electrical circuits. This is right and proper, and guarantees a minimum entitlement of learning to all. But it has meant in some cases that children are not finding out enough about their own locality. A primary school in Norfolk complained to the QCA that they were 'not allowed' to study Lord Nelson (their local hero) because the period in which he lived was not one of the alternatives offered in the Key Stage 2 Programmes of Study. Although this is strictly true, there is no ban on studying other periods as well, and the Key Stage 1 programmes certainly give scope for studying 'the lives of significant men and women'. It has already been noted that the present flexibility would allow a school to include anything it wanted in the curriculum. However, there is still a feeling that a national curriculum prevents a truly local flavour. This has come about not just from the National Curriculum itself, but from the QCA schemes of work that were originally intended as exemplars rather than schemes to be followed. Nevertheless, many schools have followed them rigidly. When the QCA Geography scheme was first published, the Llandudno Tourist Office was swamped with requests for information because it had been used as an example of a contrasting location. QCA had not thought to warn the tourist office of the impending avalanche, because it had not imagined that so many schools would follow the scheme so literally.

Local needs

The second aspect of a local setting is the particular needs and circumstances of the children themselves. There are national aims and goals, and Attainment Targets, but these may not cover all the aspirations and needs that pertain in the locality. The Leeds school performing plays about the Rivers had a need to promote inter-ethnic understanding and tolerance. The children in a very rural primary school that was surrounded by fields of vegetables were out at break one day when a tractor passed by towing a vast trailer full of turnips and one fell out and rolled into the playground. The headteacher was astonished to find that very few of the children knew what it was. They were surrounded by endless fields of turnips, and they did not know what they were. Inside the school, the curriculum was about the Incas, Chembokali, and how to form the past tense by adding 'ed'. It was not teaching the children anything about their own locality or relating to their own lives. It made the headteacher realise that she needed to change the curriculum.

Now, you might say that it would be very difficult to base a curriculum on turnips, anyway, and you might point out that the school in Leeds had a great advantage, given that city's history and rich variety of resources. The headteacher of the rural school saw it the other way. She was determined to introduce two elements:

- Knowledge and understanding about their locality;
- An appreciation of how they related to the wider world.

She added these as key elements of design in one of the 'design triangle' we discussed in Chapter 3. Teachers were asked to add this element where possible to the experiences they were designing.

In Year 1, the children were looking at 'Houses and Homes' from a geographical and historical point of view. They extended this to look at the habitats of animals. This took them into the turnip fields and they looked at the insects under the leaves and in the soil (those that had escaped the farmer's insecticides) which proved astonishing to the children. They then went a bit farther afield to a small wood that had been left along a stream; there they found more insects and evidence of small animals and birds. In their writing, these children were practising making lists, so this made the other part of the design triangle (see Figure 12.1).

Back in school, the children placed this local knowledge in a wider setting by looking up what sort of animals live in other woods, and what vegetables are grown elsewhere in the United Kingdom and abroad. They tracked where the turnips went when they left the farm, and that led to an investigation of where other vegetables came from.

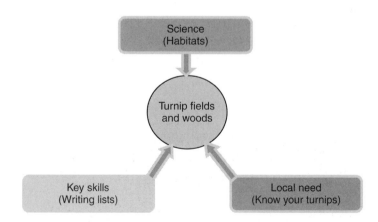

Figure 12.1 Responding to local needs

Local opportunities

As well as local needs there are also the local opportunities: all the places, people, resources and events that can be harnessed to bring learning to life. A Bristol primary school identified the need to promote civic pride as a key element of its curriculum. As it turned out, this need opened up a whole world of opportunities. The school's thinking started from the (quite correct!) assumption that it could only be ignorance that would prevent anyone being proud of Bristol. Therefore, the curriculum must allow the children to find out much more about the city. There are two ways of doing this: we could run a special unit of study on Bristol and its heritage, or we could look for ways of including it in a whole range of other learning experiences. This does not necessarily mean 'shoehorning' it into inappropriate places, but of taking account of the rich local opportunities that might otherwise be missed.

In the Bristol example, the school started by making a list of opportunities presented by the city, which became a list of experiences not to be missed. Rather like the 'Charter for Childhood', this is a list of things that should be experienced by every child reaching the age of 11. The list included famous Bristol features such as: the Suspension Bridge, SS Great Britain, Exploratory Museum, Clifton Downs and Christmas Steps (see Figure 12.2). It also included lesser known features such as the 'Floating Harbour', Cabot's ship 'The Matthew', the Observatory, and the pub of which Long John Silver was the landlord. There were also Bristol themes about which everyone should know, such as chocolate, the history of slavery, aircraft and the making of Wallace and Grommitt.

The list becomes an 'arena of opportunities'. The next part of the process was to match the forecast of possibilities to an aspect of the Programme of Study. For example, The Suspension Bridge lends itself to Design and Technology in Year 4, and History in Year 6. The Floating Harbour is ideal

Figure 12.2 Local opportunities

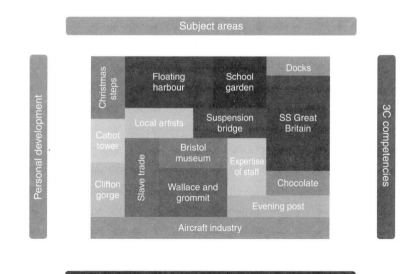

Figure 12.3 The Bristol Centre

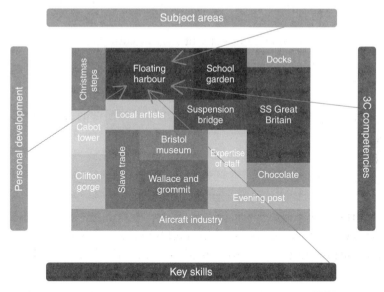

Figure 12.4 Focusing on the Floating Harbour

for Science as well as Design and Technology (flotation as well as hydraulics) and also for history. There were also possibilities for citizenship because both bridge and harbour required local decisions to be made and finance to be raised.

Having done this, the school then allocated the opportunities to each year group to ensure that none was missed. This did not prevent other year groups benefitting from the opportunity (in fact, revisiting sites and themes was specifically built into the design). The process was rather like the one in Chapter 9, but with a different centre, as seen in Figure 12.3.

This was the Bristol map of local opportunities not to be missed. What would your local map look like? The Bristol experiences then provided contexts for four elements of learning in the same way as the Chapter 8 model, as shown in Figure 12.4.

How can we get this going?

Many schools have used the Bristol method, and started with a list of local opportunities. Some have then matched these to their own local needs or aims, such as civic pride or widening horizons. These can then form a grid where local opportunities meet local needs (see Figure 12.5). This might help clarify thoughts before the design stage. At this point, some of you will be saying that it's alright to talk about Bristol with its super-rich range of opportunities, but what about my town or village? You couldn't make much of a list here! However, it is surprising how much turns up in what starts off seeming a particularly barren patch for opportunities. You don't have to have a floating harbour and suspension bridge; much can be made of turnips.

Learning outside the classroom

Many of these examples have involved going outside the classroom. Many schools became nervous about taking children out of school partly because they felt the pressure to 'get through' all of the curriculum, but did not have

	Local opportunities			
		Suspension Bridge	Slave trade	Chocolate	SS Great Britain
Local needs	Civic pride	X		X	X
	Inter-ethnic understanding		X	X	X
	Raised aspirations	X	X	X	X

Figure 12.5 Grid showing local opportunities meeting local needs

adequate time, or they were worried about health and safety. Some schools still see going outside as a recreational extra to do after the SATs, and nothing to do with the curriculum. However, there is growing evidence that children learn far more outside the classroom than they ever do inside it. Ofsted confirmed this in its 2008 Report, *Learning Outside the Classroom* (ref. 0702190) (Ofsted 2008b). This found that:

> 'Hands on' activities in a range of locations contributed much to improvements in
>
> - achievement
> - standards
> - motivation
> - personal development
> - behaviour.

The report tackled head-on the Health and Safety issue by finding that it actually improves children's safety by giving them experience outside the classroom. The key here is to teach children how to be safe in the 138 hours a week they are not at school, and not just to keep them safe during the other 30 hours. The report states that: *Experiences outside the classroom contributed significantly to 'staying safe'.*

Part of the value in being outside the classroom comes from the added interest and engagement the children feel. Part of it was that the activities are more likely to be first-hand and practical. The experiences are often more memorable and:

- *Memorable activities led to memorable learning*
- *The place where activities happened often added to their value*

These experiences were most valuable when they were built into the overall curriculum rather than being seen as one-off experiences, and interestingly, secondary schools are sometimes better than primary schools at doing this:

- *There is mixed practice in EYFS*
- *Primary schools are good at using their own grounds and the local area flexibly*

- *Secondary schools are good at promoting high quality integrated learning on day and residential visits.*

Harnessing the local community

The final part of locating national expectations in a local setting is the local community itself. This is often a resource that is not fully exploited in curriculum design.

History on Your Doorstep

The film crew is working in a residential centre for elderly people. The residents are recalling their experiences during the Second World War. Some were soldiers fighting in France, Italy and Burma. Some were evacuees. One was an air-raid warden. All had suffered the deprivations and rationing, had sheltered from bombs and seen homes destroyed and people killed. All have a story to tell and are doing so to the cameras.

The film makers are children from the primary school that backs onto the centre. There is a great deal of contact between the school and the centre. For example, the children perform plays, sing carols and take the stories they have written to read to the residents. Residents help with cooking and reading, and love to share in the life of the school. Every year, children engaged in a history topic go over to talk to the residents about their experiences during the war.

Last year some children pointed out that there were fewer residents with any memories of the war, and that 'soon they would all die out'. The children were worried that this rich source of information would be lost, so it was their idea to record this for posterity in the form of next year's class doing the same topic.

The residents were keen to take part, and the project became a major piece of work with the children keen to weave the interviews into old photographs and maps in the style of a TV documentary. The children became dedicated to this task and their creativity contributed to its success, but it was the harnessing of a local resource that made it so valuable.

We have talked about the opportunities that exist in the locality, and often the major resource is the local community itself. The contribution can come in unexpected ways, such as the compost heap in Chapter 3. We often think of local artists and writers when we invite people into school, but we often miss the person with the compost heap. The value was in the science in this case, but also in the contact with the wider community, talking to adults, and recognising that there is a wide range of people who have skills and knowledge from which we can learn. The issue for the school is often one of knowing who is out there who might help. The much more important issue is making the help an integral part of the curriculum and not a one-off sideshow.

The film in the Centre for the Elderly puts community involvement at the heart of the curriculum. It is History and ICT, as well as Key Skills, 3C Competencies and Personal Development. Much of the richness comes from the community involvement.

Many schools have drawn up their whole curriculum framework in consultation with the wider community, going beyond parents and governors and involving community groups and businesses. This has served as a good way of getting people involved and ensuring 'sign-up' to the values. It can also clarify the range of possible involvement that can then become part of the overall design. The children from Chapter 6, who ran the nail bar, had presented their business plan to the local bank manager. This would have been valuable in itself, but was made even more so because the school had primed the manager to ask the children questions about percentage differences, which built on the very bit of maths they were learning at the time. The involvement of the banks was part of a wide programme of community involvement in that school, and every bit of this was built into one or other aspect of the curriculum. This meant close liaison with the community contributors, and their willingness to tailor their contribution to the children's precise learning needs.

Pupil voice

We could not refer to the involvement of the wider community without taking account of the pupils themselves: an important part of that wider community, but also an important local community in themselves. Almost all the examples we have looked at so far have involved pupils having some degree of control of their own learning. They have developed ideas and selected lines of investigation. They have taken learning in directions that the teacher has not envisaged, and been encouraged to do so. They have made some experiences last all term that were intended to last for a day.

Children learn from each other, and strengthen the process of their own learning by learning with others (Craft, Cremin and Burnard 2008). In English primary schools, we have traditionally grouped children and asked them to work together, but have not always designed the curriculum specifically to suit this form of learning. The children learning to make an animated film in Chapter 10 were a good example of curriculum design creating a dynamic for group work, because they had each been to a different part of the course. But the value of children working together is not realised without good design. There is evidence that friends working together are more likely to engage in exploratory talk (Barnes & Todd 1995; Mercer 2000) and complete tasks more effectively (Howe & Mercer 2007; Blatchford et al. 2008), and the composition of groups is important to the design of learning. Howe and Mercer also point to the need for curriculum design to create the experiences that require children to work together with specific roles, and not just do individual tasks while sitting together.

Pupil voice is sometimes seen in terms of a formal say about learning, usually at the beginning of a topic. There is often a session where children are told that next term's topic will be the Romans and are then asked what they already know, and what they would like to find out. The second question always seems particularly hard to answer. How can you know what you don't know? This is Donald Rumsfeld territory. If the pupils truly have a voice here, then there is a danger that whole areas of learning will be missed because children had no idea that they existed, so could not say that they would like to learn them.

Much more valuable is to give children an active role as learning develops, with the scope to direct and shape it. The more open ended the learning situation, the more scope children have to direct it. The more formal and closed, the less chance they have. This also depends upon the teacher's flexibility and willingness to allow the learning to take a direction they had not considered. This willingness comes from a confidence that the key overall framework is not being distorted, but that learning is taking different pathways within this framework.

With a clear framework, teachers can make use of all that a locality offers in terms of settings, resources and people. They can place learning in the local environment and community, meet local needs and take advantage of local opportunities. They can ensure that children go to the beach and marvel at barnacles, marvel equally at compost heaps or turnips, explore the rich heritage of Bristol, or work with the elderly people on their doorstep. And children can also work together and strengthen their learning in so doing.

The framework that gives the flexibility to do these things is the one we spoke about in Chapter 9. It underpins flexibility, it enables an overview to be maintained, and it allows progress to be monitored.

It is the monitoring of progress that we shall be looking at in the next chapter.

SECTION III

How will we know if we are successful?

13 Tracking success

Studying the Villages

Year 3 have visited several villages that vary one from another and which are all different from the more urban environment of the children's school. They have collected information, taken photographs, interviewed residents, drawn maps, listed the shops and other amenities and conducted a survey of the traffic.

Back in school they are discussing their findings, and the teachers asks a series of questions of different children:

'Tell us what we saw in the last village'

'How is that different from where we live?'

'Are there any things that are the same?'

'Did you notice anything about all the villages? Think of those that were on the hill, and those by the river. And think of the maps we were looking at before we went.'

'I wonder why that was . . .'

Following the discussion, the children started sorting out the information they have collected in response to the teacher's questions.

The three key curriculum design questions have been:

- What are we trying to achieve in terms of children's learning?

- How should we organise learning to achieve this?

- How will we know whether we have been successful?

The short answer to the third question is, 'We will know we are successful if the children have learned all the things we wanted them to learn.' The long answer is about how we find that out.

Before we look at that longer answer, we need to distinguish between the two implications of the question, 'Have we been successful?' The answer hinges around whether or not the children have learned the things we intended, but one aspect is about how successful the children have been in learning, and the other aspects is about how successful our curriculum has been in promoting that learning. The first aspect is 'Assessment', the second is 'Evaluation', and the two are closely linked. You might be thinking that if the children did not learn what we intended, then the curriculum certainly wasn't successful, and vice versa. And you would be right. But there are, of course, grey areas where some children learn some things but not all, and so some bits of the curriculum might be better than others. We shall take the two aspects separately: Assessment in this chapter and Evaluation in the next.

The importance of assessment

If we don't know what children have learned already, we cannot know what they need to learn next. If we don't know what they have failed to grasp, we cannot know where they need help or support. If we have no overview of how the class is doing, we cannot shape the curriculum around their needs.

But, if we have set ourselves (or the children) a wider set of goals, then we need to take account of this wider set when we seek to find out how successful we (or the children) have been in achieving them. We have Attainment Targets and Levels for the national curriculum subjects, but we have aims in the wider areas of personal development, key skills and 3C competencies. We think these are really important, and key to preparing young people for life in the 21st century. Yet at the end of Year 6 we give them a pencil and paper test in English and Maths and base all our judgements on that.

Building assessment into design

Although the Year 6 SAT is a high-stakes and very public form of assessment, it is only a small part of an armoury of much richer assessment data on which schools can draw. Teachers spend much of their time trying to find out what the children know and understand. How many times each lesson do teachers ask questions, not because they want to find out the answer, but because they want to find out who else knows the answer too? This is all part of the process of finding out, but it is not always done in relation to the goals we originally set.

There are, of course, three key reasons why we want to find out what a child has learned:

- To make a summative judgement about the child's achievement for reporting purposes;
- To help evaluate the efficacy of the school and its curriculum;
- To decide what the child should learn next.

These forms of assessment are generally called summative, evaluative and formative. For the purposes of this chapter on curriculum design, we shall focus on the implications of the third question. It is essential to be able to evaluate the efficacy of the curriculum, so we shall look at this separately in the next chapter.

Assessment and curriculum design

There is a critical difference. Assessment is finding out what it is that a child has learned from an experience. Curriculum design is ensuring that the experience will bring about the intended learning. Both processes have to be clear about what the intended learning is; assessment in order to look for it, design in order to bring it about.

Formative assessment – only half the information we need

The process of assessment involves finding out what children know, understand and can do. This is useful information, but not sufficient in itself for curriculum design. Because if it is to be useful in curriculum design, then we also need to know what it is that children don't know, can't do, and don't understand. Because it is this that tells us what they need to learn next.

Even if you know exactly what a child knows, understands and can do, you do not necessarily know what they need to learn next. For example, if you were told that a Year 10 Maths student knew how to calculate proportional change, use symbols to the nth term, and solve simultaneous linear equations in two variables, would you know what they should learn next? What do you think it should be: Calculate dis-proportional change? Use symbols to the n+xth term? Solve simultaneous linear equations in three variables?

So, you can see that what a pupil should learn next is dependent not only on what they have learned already, but also on what they are *expected* to learn next. How do we decide what this is?

The example was taken from the Level 7 Level Description for Number and Algebra. So we could look at Level 8 to get some guidance on what to do next. (Multiply two linear expressions, solve inequalities in two variables, and sketch and interpret graphs of quadratic, cubic and reciprocal function – if you are interested. Or perhaps you already knew that.) Of course, experienced teachers do already know what it is that children need to learn next, especially in English and Maths where the National Strategies have set out progressive expectations in minute detail. But this knowledge is often held in a taken for granted way, and often bears more relation to the QCA units of work than to statutory requirements or to the wider goals we have set ourselves.

The **Level Descriptions** are only one way of deciding what the children need to learn next. Their disadvantage is that they do not take account of all the wider goals that we espouse. Their advantage is that they do provide a structure that is nationally recognised and that is probably more helpful than most people think. We shall explore this further below.

We could look at the **Programmes of Study**, but these are mainly unhelpful in determining progress because they only distinguish between the two key stages. Even comparing the programme for one key stage with the next often tells us too little about what children should learn next. Many are almost identical; for example in Geography:

> Key Stage 1: use globes, maps and plans at a range of scales
> Key Stage 2: use atlases, maps and plans at a range of scales

It is not a great help in planning progress in geography to know that in six years children should move from using a globe to using an atlas. Like the Level Descriptions, the programmes also say little about our wider goals.

In Chapter 9 we looked at the advantages of drawing up our own school **Framework of Learning Expectations**. These would set out broad expectations by stage or by year and would cover the wider goals. We shall look at this further below.

If we are to re-design the curriculum to achieve wider goals and deep learning, then we need to look again at some of our taken-for-granted assumptions about progress and expectations.

Making formative use of Level Descriptions

Like the Programmes of Study, the Level Descriptions are probably more helpful and less cluttered with detail than we think if we have not looked at them for a while. In the case of the children studying the villages, the teacher's questions made good use of the descriptions. If you look at the references to places within the descriptions, you will see that the requirements are:

- Level 1 - to **observe** the places they visit;
- Level 2 – to **describe** the places they visit;
- Level 3 – to make **comparisons** and **contrasts** between one place and another;
- Level 4 – to begin to **recognise patterns** and make **generalisations**;
- Level 5 – to give **geographical explanations** for those patterns.

If you think back to the questions the teacher asked in the example at the beginning of this chapter, you will see that they follow this progression:

- *Tell us what we saw in the last village* Description – Level 2
- *How is that different from where we live?* Contrast – Level 3
- *Are there any things that are the same?* Comparison – Level 3
- *Did you notice anything about all the villages?* Generalisation – Level 4
- *I wonder why that was . . .* Calls for an explanation – Level 5

The implications for *curriculum design* are profound. In the short term, the teacher shaped the way that different children sorted their findings: some presented descriptions, some comparison and contrasts, some explained the patterns that they had detected. Of course, the teacher was not asking children to do what they could do already, but was challenging them to take the next step. The next step is not the same for all the children. This used to be called 'differentiation' and was always a great problem to schools, more latterly it is called 'personalisation' (but the change of name has not taken away the problem!) Either way, it is shaping learning experiences in the light of what the children have already learned, and what we expect them to learn next.

The implications for design in the longer term impact more generally on the nature of the experience chosen. For example, if you were targeting children who were still learning to make cogent descriptions of places, how many villages would they have to visit in order to write a description? Yes, just one would do. But how many would they need to visit in order to make contrasts and comparisons? At least two, and those villages would need some features in common and some different. The art of the curriculum designer lies in selecting villages that make this sufficiently obvious to the young geographer.

And finally, how many villages would children have to visit before they spotted that the ones on top of the hills had the houses packed closely together, while those by the river were spread out linearly? They would probably have to go to so many that there would not be sufficient time. So the curriculum designer needs to build other resources into the experience. The children would need to look at maps and pictures, or maybe aerial photographs or videos. At this level of learning, first-hand experiences would not be enough, and secondary sources would be necessary.

The key is that the experience is designed to achieve the **level** of learning that is appropriate for these children. Yet how many times do we see Year 6 children making the most painstaking study of a village with brilliantly drawn maps and pictures and the experience ending there. However well the children describe the village, it is still a description and leaves them at Level 2. This is raised as an issue not because Levels are important in themselves, but because they help us structure learning with increasing challenge. To make comparisons and contrasts is an intellectual level above writing a description, and to make a generalisation is a further level. This is also following Bloom's taxonomy of progressively deeper learning. This is not levels for the sake of levels, but the ensuring of intellectual challenge and deep learning.

Progressively deep learning

The same process can be applied to other subjects. We have already looked at History in the context of the parish register and the persuasive citizens examples. The sequence in History is:

- Level 1 – **distinguish** between past and present;
- Level 2 – recognise that there are **reasons** why people in the past acted as they did;
- Level 3 – recognise **characteristic features** of periods they have studied;
- Level 4 – recognize **changes** within and between periods;
- Level 5 – to give **historical explanations** for those changes.

These steps will help in the processes of design and assessment. The critical distinction between Levels 1 and 2 is the introduction of reasons. The Key Stage 1 programmes suggest that children look at the lives of famous men and women in the past, so in designing the experience, it would be important to enable children to think about the reasons why these people acted as they did so that the children could be challenged at Level 2. Just talking about what the historical characters did would not be sufficient. Again, this is not just to push children to a higher level for the sake of statistics, but because it drives learning to a deeper level. In Bloom's Taxonomy, knowing the story of a famous person from the past would be at the lowest or most superficial level of learning. When a child recognises the reasons why people acted as they did, the child begins to comprehend more about history. This is Bloom's second level.

It is difficult for children to recognise characteristic features of a period at Key Stage 1, if they only study the lives of famous people. This is not a concern, because there is plenty of time in Key Stage 2 for this. But the distinction between Level 3 and 4 is a good illustration of the benefit of taking account of levels in curriculum design. One history period frequently studied in Key Stage 2 is Ancient Egypt. If we allocate this to Year 5 or 6, we would be expecting children to recognise changes within this period and give some explanations. However, it is very difficult for 10-year-old children to spot the changes in the Ancient Egyptian period. It is much easier to use this period to illustrate 'characteristic feature'; these are readily apparent to the children in the form of pyramids and mummies. The Victorian period, on the other hand, was full of easily accessible changes. So from a design point of view, it would be better to study Ancient Egypt in Years 3 or 4 where the expectation would be to recognise characteristic features (Level 3). The Victorian period would be more appropriate for Years 5 and 6 where the expectation is to recognise and explain changes (Levels 4 and 5).

Within those two periods, the focus would be on those features that best illustrate the characteristic features or the changes. This process is applicable to all parts of all subjects. It is by focusing on these expectations that we ensure that the curriculum is rigorous and challenging. This is the difference between what was seen as 'woolly' topics, and a thematic approach based on clear expectations that takes learning to the deepest levels. We need to look at all our curriculum in this light; not just considering its content, but what learning is being promoted.

A universal framework of levels

One of the reasons that the Rose Review shortened the five Key Skills to four was that this made it possible to track the skills through the existing Level Descriptions. It was then possible to devise a 'universal' framework that tracked the skills and which could be applied to all subject areas, as shown in Table 13.1.

The great advantage of this framework is that it is fairly easy to remember and apply. Few people can remember the five levels for all ten subjects, so that they tend not to be used formatively to promote progress, but we look them up at the end of term to make summative judgements. The universal framework serves as a user-friendly tool to design experiences and also to track progress. It can be kept in the mind and used 'on the hoof', as the teacher did after the village study. All of the criteria exist in the present Level Descriptions, so do not involve deviating from the present standards. The change is to focus on the skills aspect of the Level Descriptions rather than the content.

We have already looked in some detail at how this would apply in History and Geography. For example, if children are able to describe the village in the study, then they are challenged to notice similarities and differences (Level 3) and then to notice the pattern to these differences (Level 4) and eventually explain the reason why villages at the tops of hills are clustered close together while those along the river are spread out (Level 5).

Table 13.1 Universal framework of levels

	Level 1	Level2	Level 3	Level 5	Level 5
Investigate	Observe things around them	Describe and order their observations	Make comparisons and contrasts	Make generalisations and detect patterns	Give subject-appropriate explanations for these
Create and develop	Recognise simple features	Make suggestions	Give reasons and develop own ideas	Decide a course of action and carry it out	Take account of variable factors in action
Evaluate	Recognise simple features	Suggest improvements	Modify and refine	Analyse in relation to use	Consider wider implications
Communicate	Communicate in simple terms	Make explanations using appropriate language	Communicate in a subject-specialist way	Use and combine a range of methods to communicate more complex ideas	Communicate more sophisticated ideas in clear and persuasive ways

The structure applies in different ways to all subject areas, and the differences are in part the differences in the subject areas themselves. The references are already in the present Level Descriptions, so this is not introducing a new element, but making sense of a rather confused system. The one change that was necessary to make the framework apply universally is in Science where the present expectation is that children will compare and contrast at Level 2 and make generalisations at Level 3. There is no reason for this to apply differently in Science, and it is only different because the Levels were written originally by different subject groups in isolation. Changing the science expectation does not materially alter the overall standard, and, indeed, it keeps the key elements of Levels 4 and 5, but makes them more comprehensible.

The way the generic framework would apply to a Science experiment is that children would be able to

- describe in some detail the changes over time in the plants they were growing (Level 2);
- compare the plants near the window with the ones near the wall (Level 3);
- generalise that the farther the plant was from the window the paler its leaves or the thinner it was (Level 4);
- explain that the reason for this is that the more intense light near the window increased the rate of photosynthesis (Level 5).

In other subjects, the framework fits with the existing Levels. Many schools might wish to go into greater detail in English and Maths, and there is already extensive guidance to be used. Using the Key Competencies outlined in Chapter 9 as the basis of curriculum design, rather than all of English and Mathematics, may seem to be too thin to ensure proper standards in these key subjects, especially as these are the ones for which there will be a national test. However, many schools have found that adapting the expectations to make them more manageable for both teachers and children has had the effect of raising standards rather than lowering them. These are the standards as measured by national tests as well as those seen by the teacher.

The school whose pupils were in the wood looking at stars (the school with 95 per cent Level 5 writers) had only average standards when it started its curriculum journey. It was struggling to get through all of the National Literacy Strategy so left some bits out, keeping a close eye on SAT scores for fear that they would fall. In fact, the scores rose, so they cut even more out of the Strategy. The scores rose again. By the time the school was not doing the Strategy at all, its scores could not have been higher. Of course, it did not abandon the structure of the National Strategy without putting something else in its place. But its own strategy was much more manageable.

Making it manageable

The danger of too extensive a structure of expectations is that they all get built into curriculum design so that it gets overloaded. Teachers try to cope with the overload by teaching more directly and giving less time for children to explore ideas and practise skills. This results in children being stuck at Bloom's first level, rather than progressing to deeper levels. The interesting thing is that if a smaller key range of expectations is selected, and the children are given more time to develop skills within these contexts, they are likely to explore these other expectations anyway. The work of Charles Desforges and Richard Fox (2002) is illuminating here. In seeking to map learning, he found that children frequently learned things not on the 'agenda' at all. Sometimes the learning was 'unlocked' by the learning of a new concept in a seemingly unrelated area. This is because learning is not the simple linear progression of our curriculum plans, but a more complex interrelated network of progression where one thing leads to a variety of others.

It is therefore important that when schools draw up their Framework of Learning Expectations, they avoid the temptation to put in as much as they possibly can. If it becomes too long and detailed, it will cease to be a useful framework that guides learning even deeper, and will become instead an obstacle course of ground to be covered and hoops to jump through that actually impedes progress.

A Framework of Learning Expectations

Chapter 9 put forward the idea of a framework that would set out expectations by stage or year group for:

- Personal development
- Key skills

- 3C competencies
- Subject areas

Each of these aspects fed into the design of learning experiences for the class.

The Framework sets out the expectations by stage or by year group (or whatever grouping the school uses within its curriculum arrangements). All of these expectations feed into the year group curriculum, as shown in Figure 13.1.

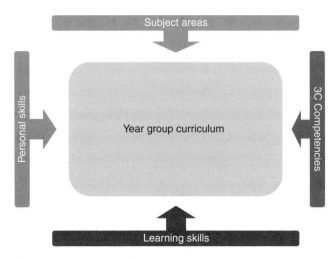

Figure 13.1 The year group curriculum

Possible progressive stages for the first three of these, and Chapter 9 looked at the way Key Subject Concepts and Key Subject Skills could be the basis for curriculum design within the subject areas.

Because the overall Framework of Expectations is the basis for design, it also becomes the basis for checking that the expectations have been achieved. If these are the expectations, then these are also the things we need to look for.

Looking for evidence of a particular expectation being achieved becomes much easier if that expectation has been built into the design in the first place. The teacher does not have to wonder if the children have noticed that there is a pattern to all the villages they have looked at, because that was the whole point of the experience. What she does have to notice is which children were able to do this and which were still at the comparison stage. These are the notes that the teacher keeps to feed into the next experience.

Some schools have tabulated their frameworks alongside children's names so that a quick record can be kept of who has met which expectation. This becomes the basis for personalising learning. This need not be arduous, so long as the framework was kept manageable in the first place. The advantage of such a system is that it is simple and manageable. The dangers are that experiences could end up being designed just to get some ticks in the box rather than to deepen children's learning, and that once the box has been ticked the skill is considered to have been mastered and not need revisiting.

The complexity of skills

This would, indeed be a danger because skills exist in several dimensions. Chapter 9 set out some ways on which expectations about skills can be set out in stages. The universal framework in this chapter sets out expectations about skills in Levels. Around the country, there are countless 'skills ladders' and skills progression routes have been charted and are in use. But there are other ways in which skills develop.

If we take one skill like problem-solving, we could look at it in three ways:

- First, we could take the skills-ladder approach and pull the skill out into steps or stages. These might be, in ascending order: identify problems, isolate factors, take account of multiple factors, suggest solutions, test solutions and so on.

- Second, we could look at the sort of problems that need to be solved. These provide a second form of progression: starting by solving simple problems and ending by solving very complex ones. The procedure for finding a solution might be the same in every case. What changes is the increasing complexity of the problems.

- Third, we could take account of the context in which the problem is being solved. A child (or adult!) may be quite capable of solving a problem with some help, but not by themselves. The progression might be one of increasing independence in the use of a skill.

The first example here is a good illustration of why many people are suspicious of skills ladders. They argue that breaking a skill down into its component parts may seem logical, but skills are not learned like that nor are they used like that. Skills are developed and used holistically and not as separate parts. This is why the Universal Framework of Levels attempted to keep each description as a skill in itself, rather than only part of one.

A subject example from the National Curriculum would be the Level 4 expectation to control variables in an experiment. If the experiment is rolling two cars down a slope, then it is fairly easy to control the variables, and most 9-year-olds can do it. If the experiment is to find the Higgs Boson in the Hadron Collider, then there will be few people in the world able to exert such control. It is not the ladder of the skill that needs extending to take account of this – it is the sheer extent and complexity of the experiment.

The Hadron Collider also illustrates the fact that skills are often used within a team rather than individually. There may be no one in the world with the skill to run that experiment by themselves. It is only by working as a team that it can be done.

It is possible to put together the two dimensions of complexity and independence as vertical and horizontal axes, as shown in Figure 13.2.

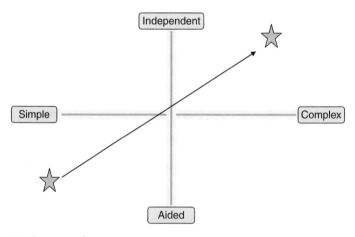

Figure 13.2 The axes of progress

The line of progress here is from solving simple problems with some help to solving more complex ones independently. But the line of progress is seldom as straight as the one depicted here. A child may become independent in simple situations, but still need help in more complex ones, so the line of progress may zigzag at first. Some of us may even continue to zigzag through life.

The impact of context is seen across the range of skills and attributes.

A range of contexts for skills

It might not even be the increasing complexity of the problems that is the mark of progress. It could also be the range of types of problems that is important. To be better at a skill is to be able to perform it in an increasingly diverse range of situations. A child may be able to work well in a football team, but not when the team is engaged in Science. Another child is creative in Music, but not in Design and Technology. It may be even more specific than that: being able to perform a skill in one aspect of subject but not another. Not because they are more complex, but because they are different. Progression would, therefore, be seen as a greater range of performance.

Keeping track of this sort of complexity is obviously difficult. We need not only to be aware of the level of performance, but also the range of situations. This goes beyond ticking a level in a box.

The Subject Areas

In Chapter 9, we looked at three aspects of the Subject Areas that might appear in the Framework of Expectations:

- The Key Skills
- Key Concepts
- The Breadth of Learning

The *Key Subject Skills* are taken care of by the generic set of Levels described above, so there is a good method for establishing how successfully these are being developed.

The *Key Concepts* are not necessarily aspects that can be graded in the same way. Like some aspects of the skills, the concepts are deepened and strengthened by being explored in an increasing range of contexts. For example, the Key History Concept that 'technology impacts on society' might have been explored in the contexts of the Railways in Victorian times, but also the invention of the plough in Assyria, and aviation in the 20th century. It would not be possible (or necessary, or even desirable) to attribute levels to this deepening, but the increasing depth would be recorded within the Framework.

The *Breadth of Learning* is also not a matter of level or stage, but of increasing range. Again, this is recorded within the Framework.

For all three of these aspects, the teacher will note whether the expectations were met or not. This will provide formative information for designing the next experience, and will also enable the teacher and school to reflect upon the efficacy of the design.

This process is evaluation, and is the subject of the next chapter.

14 Keeping an overview: evaluation

The Supermarket Visit

A class of Year 1 children from an inner city school was taken to the local supermarket as part of a Maths project on money and prices that involved setting up their own supermarket in the classroom. The class is normally very well behaved and the teacher had no qualms about taking them on the visit. There was extra supervision from teaching assistants and the risk assessments had been completed. What could go wrong?

Once in the supermarket, the normally well-behaved children started running about, screaming and pulling things off the shelves. The teacher was shocked, and when she had finally restored order and rounded up the children, she vowed never to take them to a supermarket ever again.

Her evaluation of this part of the curriculum was understandably negative.

Have we been successful?

The key assessment question is whether the children have been successful in learning what was intended. The key evaluation question is whether we have been successful in designing a curriculum that has enabled them to learn those things.

The key concern about moving to a more flexible model of curriculum design is how the school can be sure that at the end of the whole process all the flexibly designed learning experiences will add up to a coherent, worthwhile, broad and balanced set of learning that will achieve the aims originally set. How will we keep an overview if teachers have the flexibility to design and shape learning experiences as they go along?

The Framework of Expectations also serves this purpose. By setting out a structure of expectations within which teachers have the flexibility to design learning experiences that meet the developing needs of the children, the Framework ensures that all these experiences add up to a coherent whole. It does so in two ways: by giving some assurance in advance that the curriculum will be coherent (quality assurance) and by providing a way of checking that the curriculum as experienced by the children actually is building towards coherence (quality control).

But what was the intention of taking Year 1 to the supermarket, and why did they behave in such an unexpected way? In discussing the incident, the school worked out what was going on. Children's behaviour is contextually related. If they are socially competent, they know that they behave one way in school assembly and another way in the playground. Unfortunately, these children seemed to have learned that the way you behave in a supermarket is to run around and grab things from the shelves. So was taking them to a supermarket a mistake never to be repeated? Not if some of your aims for these children is to do with their social skills. They need to go to the supermarket many times to learn how it can be done. Once the teacher had realised this, and had recovered from her trauma, back she went – but with small groups this time. This is evaluation in action.

Quality assurance

By setting out expectations across the primary stage, the Framework is building in the breadth, balance and progressive challenge that we seek. By enabling links to be made between one piece of learning and another, the Framework is also helping to ensure coherence. If the Framework is followed, then there is some assurance that all the experiences created will add up to the coherent and worthwhile whole. This could be seen as 'Quality Assurance'. But as the experiences are developed within the Framework, it also acts as a system of quality control.

Quality control

In Chapter 9, it was pointed out that in designing the learning experiences, the teacher will make a record of those aspects she intends to include. But as the experiences evolve and conclude, the teacher will revise that record in the light of:

- Intended aspects that were not actually included after all;
- Aspects that were included, but were not originally intended;
- Aspects that were included but which the children, or some groups of children, did not actually learn;

This record then becomes the basis for planning the next experience: including the things left out, bringing in new things and going over old things that were not fully learned. This developing design gives the flexibility to respond to assessment information; it is 'Assessment for Learning' in action. It is also the record of what has actually been learned and so is the basis for ongoing evaluation.

This gives a method of tracking individual pupils as well as tracking the whole class. It also gives a method for identifying those experiences from which children did not learn as much as was expected, and those experiences from which it turned out that they learned much more. This information feeds back into curriculum design as a formative evaluation (see Figure 14.1).

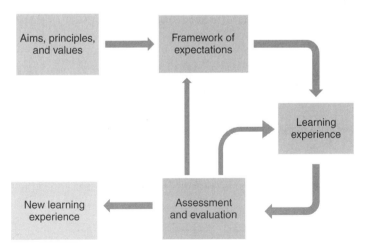

Figure 14.1 The evaluation process

The information gained from assessment and evaluations may inform three parts of the process:

- The design of the next learning experience will be based upon what the children have learned in the present one.

- The present learning experience may be amended as is goes along in the light of ongoing assessment. Or it may be decided to amend it before using it again, or never to use it again.

- There might be implications for the Framework itself. It might have been too ambitious, or not ambition enough. Or the Framework might need amending for a particular class, or group that had needs different from the usual.

Keeping the overview

In primary schools it is usually the headteacher who has overall oversight of the curriculum, or it could be a deputy or curriculum co-ordinator. (The Introduction to this book argued that as the curriculum is the whole raison d'être of the school, then oversight should be at the very highest level.) Whoever has this role, the responsibility is twofold:

- To impact on the designs *before* they are carried out to help ensure that they are appropriate to the intended learning;

- To review the *outcome* of the experiences to see what was learned and what was not and how this needs to be fed into the next stage of design.

The second of these helps the 'feedback loops' in the above diagram. The class teacher will be able to feedback into the design of the next experience, and amend the present one, but amending the Framework for the school or next class will be done at a senior level.

Most headteachers or co-ordinators look at curriculum plans in advance of their implementation, but most do this from the point of view of compliance, and few do it from the point of view of quality. To follow the flexible approach to providing challenge and deep learning that has been put forward in this book, it might be helpful to ask the questions, as per the checklist in Figure 14.2, when reviewing in advance an aspect of curriculum design.

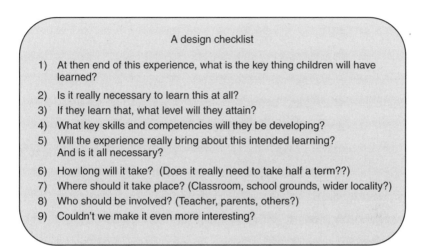

Figure 14.2 A design checklist

Each of these questions should impact on the design. Let's take the points one by one.

1 If it is not clear what the key learning is, then this needs to be clarified. What is the point of doing this at all? The clarification often alters the design for the better.

2 Why is this piece of learning being included in the curriculum? Is it a requirement of the National Curriculum, an Essential Experience of childhood or the locality, an attempt to widen the children's understanding? Or is it something we could not bother to do at all. We need to be rigorous here.

3 If you can't find this piece of learning in any of the Level Descriptions, then you need to wonder why you are including it. If you can't find it in the Generic Framework of Levels, it means that you are not including any key skills. This is a key question in terms of challenge and rigour. And it

has profound implications for the design. Is Level 4 a sufficient challenge for all the children? What if our assessments show that some are Level 4 already? What will they be learning? How can we change the design to take account of this?

4 Have we included roots as well as leaves? Are these building on skills already acquired? What about aspects of personal development?

5 This point is often missed. There is a clear learning objective, and an engaging experience, but the two do not always match. However long the children take part in the experience, they would never achieve the objectives. There needs to be rigour here before the design is implemented. We also need to ask whether *all* of the experience is necessary. Does some seem unnecessary or irrelevant?

6 Ideally the design will not be within a timeframe, but will be focused on the outcome. Nevertheless, the teacher will have some sort of timeframe in mind and this needs rigorous challenge.

7 This is the opportunity for widening the experience. Couldn't we take the children out of school? To a museum, a field trip, or just engage in some practical, first-hand activity. Is it best as a series of lessons, or could it be an event or part of the routines?

8 This could also widen the experience. Does it just have to be the teacher? Could parents be involved, local experts, outside visitors, teachers from other classes? (Does anyone have a compost heap?)

9 All curriculum design discussions should end (or start!) with asking how we can make it as exciting as possible for the children.

These are all questions that could be asked by the headteacher or curriculum co-ordinator looking through designs. They are also questions that could frame the curriculum design meetings between teachers. If we can be really clear about questions 1 to 4, then we can start thinking about the questions of 'quality' in 5 to 9. This will enable the process to be about curriculum design rather than curriculum planning, and will focus on the quality of children's learning experiences and not just on what they will learn.

If the children achieve the expectations in the Framework, then the curriculum will have been successful in promoting its aims. And if the Framework is broad and coherent, then the curriculum will be so too, so long as the experiences continue to promote the Framework's expectations. This is why the evaluation process must be continuous and the feedback must impact on design.

The overall model of interactive evaluation

The main purpose of evaluation is to help get the design process right. So the evaluation must interact with the design process to be effective. It must feed back into the present experience to shape its development and the next experience to ensure it builds on what has just been learned, and also feeds back to the Framework itself to ensure that it is relevant to each group of children (see Figure 14.3).

High quality design is the most important part of quality assurance. If we get this right, then we can be sure that we shall be successful.

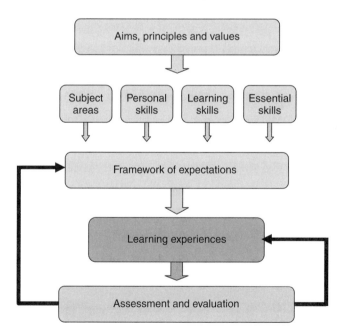

Figure 14.3 Keeping an overview

Answering the question

So the way we shall know whether we have been successful is bound up in the Framework we use for design. Although it allows flexibility, it does not leave things to chance. There is some assurance of the quality of the curriculum as well as a system for controlling its quality as it develops.

This is a process of intelligent curriculum design.

The final question is: How can we get it all going in our schools?

SECTION IV

How do we get from here to there?

15 Getting from here to there

The Roman Feast

The Romans, clad in togas, are sprawled on cushions, eating lazily from the wide array of dishes set out on low tables. Soldiers stand guard with helmets and swords. As the feast progresses, servants circulate with large jugs, filling the diners' cups with orange juice. Orange juice might not have been the drink of choice for most feasting Romans, but these are not your typical Romans. They are from Year 3, they have cooked all the food themselves, made their own togas and headgear, and the servants are their parents. This is the culmination of a study of Ancient Rome.

In a nearby classroom, the parallel Year 3 class has also been studying Ancient Rome, but their approach has been much more traditional, involving reference books, worksheets and much writing.

A common reaction to the approaches set out in this book is that they are, indeed, the best way for children to learn – but would be very difficult in my school. Headteachers frequently think that their staff would find it too difficult to cope with flexibility: 'They have been trained to follow the National Strategies and all they can do is teach a three-part lesson.' Teachers often say that although they would love to teach this way, their headteacher wouldn't let them: 'We've got to follow set lesson plans, and are not allowed to deviate from them.' Everyone blames the teacher training institutions for not turning out teachers as curriculum designers. The training institutions point out that they are constrained by the Training and Development Agency (TDA) targets, and that if they send out students who can't teach a three-part lesson, then headteachers complain.

And then there is a worry about the impact on SAT scores or what Ofsted or the SIP will say.

In the middle of all this are the children. They deserve the very best curriculum we can lay before them. The curriculum should be a feast of experiences, and one that excites their imaginations and nourishes their intellectual development. So the children should not be constrained by such institutional issues. If we know what is the best curriculum for the children, then that is the one we should provide.

But is it alright to do it? How do we get our teachers to do it, if we don't think they can? Or how do we do it ourselves if we are not sure where to start? And do we have to throw out all our curriculum plans and start again? And is there any point in doing anything now when the whole curriculum is being reviewed and we shall have to do what we are told anyway? Let's take these questions one by one, in more or less reverse order.

Is there any point in starting now?

There are always reasons for starting something later, but none that outweigh the benefits to the children of starting right now. This is their only chance at school and we cannot let the time tick away. If we believe that this is the best way for children to learn, then that is the way they should be learning now.

Although the National Curriculum is being reviewed as this book is being published, don't forget that:

- The National Curriculum is only part of the whole curriculum.
- The present one gives schools a huge amount of flexibility and can be designed in any way.
- The new one promises even more flexibility.
- If the new National Curriculum turns out to be light on skills, competencies and personal development, we would want to have a structure for these anyway.

- The new one will not be introduced until 2013, and when it is you can incorporate it into your design.
- In all countries, the school's role is to turn the national curriculum into learning experiences for the children. They need to design experiences that meet the children's needs and circumstances, which are rooted in their localities, and which build on their previous learning.

Do we have to throw out all our curriculum plans and start again?

Not only do we not need to do this, it would be an ill-advised strategy. The most sensible way to start is to take one piece of learning that was planned for next term and rethink it in terms of the principles outlined in this book. In the previous chapter, we set out a list of questions that a curriculum designer might ask to ensure that a planned experience would effectively promote the intended learning. It would be good to apply these to an already planned piece of learning. How would you change it in the light of these questions? Is the learning intention clear? Is it something the children really need to learn? Is it at the right level of demand for these children? Does it build in any 'root' skills? We can then go on to the 'quality' questions about the experience: time, place, people and the very nature of the experience.

The outcome might be to refine the planned piece of learning or to add some extra skills or might be to approach it in an entirely different way. This will have some implications for other aspects of existing planning (e.g. some aspects of Maths could be included in History, and so taken out of a later part of the Maths programme) but it does not mean that it all has to be thrown out.

After one such revision, another can be designed, and then another. The advantage of this gradual approach is that we can learn as we go along and refine our approach to design. As Figure 15.1 shows, the existing curriculum can be gradually transformed into a new set of experiences.

With each new experience, there will be less left in the existing one until it has been transformed (see Figure 15.2). Many schools see this as a safer way than throwing everything out and starting again. The impact can be monitored as you go along and necessary adjustments made. The problem

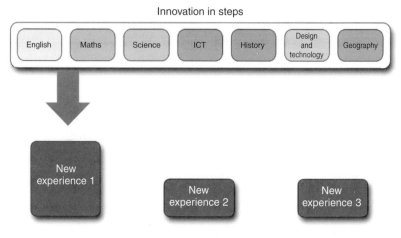

Figure 15.1 Innovation in steps – new experience 1

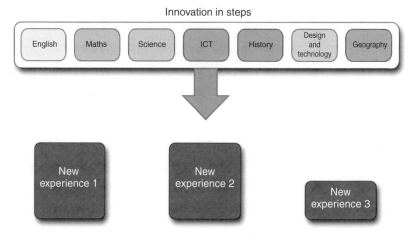

Figure 15.2 Innovation in steps – new experience 2

often comes in the form of customer resistance. Children are often reluctant to go back to less exciting ways!

Where do we start?

In one sense, we start as above, by changing one thing at a time. But in reality, there needs to be a solid background to the new design. Early chapters of this book pointed to the need to be clear about overall aims, principles and values so that curriculum design can reflect and embrace these. This is also

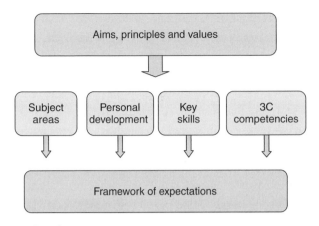

Figure 15.3 Starting the process

the best place to start as a school to ensure that the new approach is understood and 'bought into'. It was suggested that drawing up aims, principles and values was a process that should draw in parents, governors, children and the wider community. This gives the approach weight and legitimacy, and can give confidence to the school and teachers.

From the set of aims, principles and values comes the Framework of Expectations that we dealt with in Chapter 9. It is when this Framework has been established that the process of design can be firmly rooted in a structure of expectations. Without this, teachers would be designing new experiences in response to the ten questions, but not really knowing what should go into the design. The Framework needs sections on personal, learning and essential skills and on the subject areas.

So the process of getting this going could be set out in a diagram as in Figure 15.3.

With the Framework completed, the process of curriculum design is ready to start. We are now ready to ask whether we can actually work in this way.

How do we get people to work in this way?

The best place to start is to involve people in the process of drawing up the aims, values, principles and framework. This goes a long way towards developing the level of understanding and commitment that will be needed to work in a different way. The next step is to get started.

Many schools find the stumbling block is getting *all* the staff to commit to a new approach. However, many schools have shown that this is not essential. In the school in the opening example, there was reluctance on the part of many staff to change their approach, while others were keen to get going. Instead of trying to persuade, or require, everyone to change, the headteacher let people do things in their own way. Hence, one Year 3 class was having the Roman Feast in the hall, while children in the parallel class were filling in their worksheets.

You can imagine the impact. The Year 3 children in their classroom looked out at the feast and demanded to know why they couldn't dress up and have a feast too. Moreover, their parents asked the same question. So there was pressure to adopt the new approach. The clincher came when displays of the Roman work started going up around the school. The work from the 'Roman Feasters' was clearly of much better quality than the perfunctory offerings of the traditional workers. Not only that, but the children were keener and more engaged, and their behaviour was much better. By the end of the year, the school's tracking data had made the case complete. The Roman Feasters had surged ahead in English and Maths as well as in the range of other aims and skills. By that time, the reluctant teachers had seen the light.

In school after school, the experience has been that teachers find this approach much less difficult than they, or their headteachers, expect. This is also true for newly qualified teachers, despite doubts about the nature of their training. In many schools, it is the youngest teachers who are driving the reform. By starting small and gradually building up, teachers can build confidence and experience and can gradually develop the experiences they design in ever more creative ways. By having a clear framework within which to work, teachers find the process of design far less open-ended and daunting. Curriculum design meetings can focus on quality and excitement. After a while, many teachers say that this is what they came into the profession for.

This positive feeling comes from several aspects of the approach. Teachers like seeing children learn; that **is** what they came into the profession for. The children are more engaged and interested in their work, so there are fewer problems with reluctant learners or with behaviour. And after a while teachers realise that there is far less planning to do in the new approach. Once more open-ended situations have been set up and children have independence to work within these situations, then the learning rolls forward without the same level of planning. Teachers have to be responsive to developing situations and perhaps think more 'on their feet', but there are far fewer formal lessons to be planned. If you think back to the parish register example, once the teacher had come up with the idea and photocopied the pages of the register, there was little more to do by way of planning. Instead of planning lessons for three days, she came up with one good idea and then gave the children the independence to follow it. Her role was one of support and providing ongoing challenge ('How do you know that is the right explanation?') rather than planning each individual step of learning. Very few teachers do not prefer to work in this way.

Can something that seems easier and better to the teachers, and that the children enjoy more, actually be any good? Surely medicine can't be effective if it tastes good?

But what will Ofsted say?

In Chapter 5, we looked at the various constraints that schools perceive as stopping them from being more creative in their approach. One was the impact on the Year 6 SAT scores. It was pointed out that the experience of hundreds of schools in QCA's 'Co-development groups' was that a different approach to curriculum design actually improved standards in English and Maths, and improved scores in national tests. This was confirmed by the Ofsted Report into curriculum innovation (*Curriculum Innovation in Schools* 2008 Ref. 070097) (Ofsted 2008a), which found that 93 per cent of innovative schools increased their SAT scores.

This led to Ofsted changing its criterion for judging the curriculum to be '*The school may be at the forefront of innovative curriculum design . . .*' So, this answers the next perceived constraint of 'What will Ofsted say?' If you are successfully innovative, Ofsted will say you are outstanding. Within the QCA group of co-development schools, well over half were deemed 'outstanding' by Ofsted in terms of their curriculum.

An unintended, but very welcome, consequence is often in terms of parental involvement. In the school holding the Roman Feast, parents had hardly ever entered the building before the curriculum change, even though the school had tried very hard to encourage them. Looking back, the school realised that the parents had seen no role for themselves in the fairly formal lessons that were the prevalent way of learning. Most of these parents had been unsuccessful at school themselves and felt that they had little to offer. As soon as learning became more active, parents started getting involved. The home–school partnership improved and this contributed to even better learning. Things started spiralling upwards.

A strong moral purpose

This book has been about trying to create the very best primary curriculum. This is much more than trying to please Ofsted or increase the SAT scores. These are outcomes to the school's advantage, and we have been talking about a much higher and more moral purpose: trying to give children the very best start to their lives.

With a wider set of aims and values built into the curriculum, the impact will be much wider than the traditional measures and systems of accountability. The impact will be on children's personal development, and the ways they see themselves in relation to the wider world. It will impact on the children's own attitudes, values and principles, and on the way they operate in society as global citizens.

The curriculum will give them deeper knowledge and understanding within the subject areas, so that opportunities will open up to them as they get older, so that they can pursue their studies further. It will equip them with the skills they need to live their lives successfully in the 21st century. It will make them life-long learners.

It will give them the basis they need to enter adulthood with the confidence, the ability and the desire to make the world a better place.

If we achieve that, then we shall truly have a world-class curriculum.

Postscript
A world-class curriculum

A Flood of Ideas

A primary school in India is situated alongside one of the upper tributaries of the Ganges. This river had seldom flooded until recently, but climate change is melting the glaciers and floods are becoming common. The school made this a topic of study. The children consulted village elders to gain their wisdom about how they coped with previous floods. They took measurements and constructed high platforms where school equipment could be stored above flood level. They made lifejackets out of plastic water bottles, and took courses on resuscitation. They lobbied the local government about flood defences, and started a website to bring public attention to their plight. Their work involved maths, science, geography, technology, communication, citizenship and a whole range of leaves. It was rooted in their own experience and their own locality, it had a strong real and moral purpose and the children had a compelling emotional commitment.

Their story is now on the website of the British Council (www.britishcouncil.org/savinglives). These are truly global citizens.

The Introduction to this book referred to the notion of a 'World Class Curriculum', and suggested that there might be a set of principles and approaches that would take a curriculum way beyond the ordinary and sufficient, and make it truly 'world-class'. These principles and approaches would apply in any country whatever the national curriculum. They take

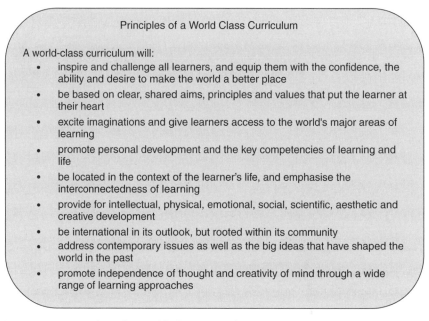

Figure PS.1 Principles of a world-class curriculum

learning beyond the national and approach the universal. This is the way to create a curriculum for global citizens.

These world-class principles would be about the way the country's national curriculum is turned into learning experiences for children that are exciting and uplifting, that recognise the individuality of every child, and which encourage their development as human beings.

If we were to pull together the strands that run through this book, certain principles stand out, as can be observed in Figure PS.1.

These are a set of aspirations that will guide the development of curriculum change within a school. They could also become the touchstone or benchmark by which a curriculum is evaluated, and by which schools could work together in partnership to create and endorse such a curriculum.

The Curriculum Foundation (a not-for-profit organisation) is developing the notion of professional peer evaluation against such principles as a way of promoting a World Class Curriculum. You can find out more at www.curriculumfoundation.org. The process of curriculum design should be a corporate one, a matter of professional co-operation. Working with other schools is not only professionally rewarding, it is the best way of extending our own ideas, developing the creativity of our approach, and designing the very best curriculum we can set before the children, wherever they are in the world.

At the beginning of this book, we set out the ambition that the curriculum should equip every young person to enter adulthood with the confidence, the ability and the desire to make the world a better place. We can achieve that ambition if we ourselves are ambitious about what the curriculum can achieve. Through our design, we can unleash the full power of the curriculum and make learning irresistible.

References

Alexander, R. (ed.) (2009). *Children, their world, their education*. Abingdon: Routledge.

Ananiadoui, K., & Claro, M. (2009). *21st century skills and competences for new millennium learners in OECD countries*. OECD Education Working Paper, No. 41. doi: 10.1787/218525261154.

Anderson, L. W., & Krathwohl, D. R. (eds) (2001). *A taxonomy for learning, teaching, and assessing: A revision of Bloom's taxonomy of educational objectives*. New York: Longman.

Barnes, D. & Todd, F. (1995). *Communication and learning revisited: Making meaning through talk*. Portsmouth, NH: Boynton/Cook Publishers Inc.

Bennett S. N. (1976). *Teaching styles and pupil progress*. London: Open Books.

Blatchford, P., Hallam, J., Ireson, J., Kutnik, P. with Creech, A. (2008). Classes, groups and transitions: Structures for teaching and learning. *Primary Review Research Briefings*, 9/2, Cambridge: University of Cambridge.

Bloom, B. (ed.) (1956). *The taxonomy of educational objectives. The classification of educational goals. Handbook I: Cognitive domain*. New York: Susan Fauer Company.

Bruner, J. S. (1966). *Towards a theory of instruction*. Cambridge, MA: Harvard University Press.

CCEA. (2003). *The revised Northern Ireland primary curriculum foundation stage*. Belfast: Author.

Craft A., Cremin, T., & Burnard, P. (eds) (2008). *Creative learning 3-11*. Stoke-on-Trent: Trentham Books.

Craft, A., Gardner, H., & Claxton, G. (eds) (2007). *Creativity, wisdom and trusteeship*. Thousand Oaks, CA: Corwin Press.

Desforges, C., & Fox, R. (eds) (2002). *Teaching and learning.* Oxford: Blackwell.

Facer, K., Furlong, R., & Sutherland, R. (2003). *Screenplay: Children and computing in the home.* London: Routledge

Gardner, H. (1999). *The disciplined mind.* London: Penguin Books.

Goswami, U. (2008). *Cognitive development: The learning brain.* Psychology Press, Taylor & Francis.

Goswami, U., & Bryant, P. (2007). Children's cognitive development and learning. *Primary Review Research Briefings*, 2/1a. Cambridge: University of Cambridge.

Hargreaves, D. (2006). *A new shape for learning.* London: SSAT.

Heppell, S., Chapman, C., Millward, R., Constable, M., & Furness, J. (2004). *Building Learning Futures.* London: CABE/RIBA.

HMI. (1976). *Primary schools in England.* London: HMSO.

HMI. (1985). *The curriculum from 5 to 16.* London: HMSO.

Howe, C., & Mercer, N. (2007). Children's social development: Peer interaction and classroom learning. *Primary Review Research Briefings*, 2/1b. Cambridge: University of Cambridge.

Immordino-Yang, M. H., & Damasio, A. R. (2007). We feel, therefore we learn: The relevance of affective and social neuroscience to education. *Mind, Brain and Education*, 1(1), 3–10.

Katzir, T., & Pare-Blagoev, J. (2006). Applying cognitive neuroscience research to education: The case of literacy. *Educational Psychologist*, 41(1), 53–74.

Laevers, F. (1998). Understanding the world of objects and of people: Intuition as the core element of deep level learning. *International Journal of Educational Research*, 29(1), 69–85.

Lave, J., & Wenger, E. (1991). *Situated learning: Legitimate peripheral participation.* Cambridge: Cambridge University Press.

Marton, F., & Saljo, R. (2008). *Deep and surface approaches to learning.* Sweden: University of Gothenburg.

Mercer, N. (2000). *Words and minds: How we use language to think together.* London: Routledge.

Ofsted. (2008a). *Curriculum in innovative schools* (ref: 070097). London: Ofsted.

Ofsted. (2008b). *Learning outside the classroom* (ref: 0702190). London: Ofsted.

Ofsted. (2009). *Twenty outstanding primary schools* (ref: 070170). London: Ofsted.

Pahl, K. (2005). Narrative spaces and multiple identities. In Marsh, J. (ed.), *Popular culture, new media and digital literacy in early childhood.* Abingdon: RoutledgeFalmer.

Peters, R. S., & Hirst, P. H. (1971). *The logic of education.* London: Routledge & Kegan Paul.

Piaget, J. (1969). *The mechanisms of perception.* London: Routledge & Kegan Paul.

Robinson, K. et al. (1999). *All our futures.* National Advisory Committee on Creative and Cultural Education. London: HMSO.

Vygotsky, L. S. (1978). *Mind in society: The development of higher psychological processes.* Cambridge, MA: Harvard University Press.

Wolfe, P. (2010). *Brain matters.* Alexandria, VA: ASCD Books.

Index